The Arab Spring

Other Books of Related Interest:

Opposing Viewpoints Series

America's Global Influence

Democracy

Libya

The Taliban

At Issue Series

Does the World Hate the US?

Foreign Oil Dependence

Is Foreign Aid Necessary?

The Occupy Movement

Current Controversies Series

Espionage and Intelligence

The Iranian Green Movement

Islamophobia

"Congress shall make no law . . . abridging the freedom of speech, or of the press."

First Amendment to the US Constitution

The basic foundation of our democracy is the First Amendment guarantee of freedom of expression. The Opposing Viewpoints series is dedicated to the concept of this basic freedom and the idea that it is more important to practice it than to enshrine it.

OPPOSING
VIEWPOINTS®
SERIES

The Arab Spring

Margaret Haerens and Lynn M. Zott, Book Editors

GREENHAVEN PRESS
A part of Gale, Cengage Learning

GALE
CENGAGE Learning·

Detroit • New York • San Francisco • New Haven, Conn • Waterville, Maine • London

Elizabeth Des Chenes, *Director, Publishing Solutions*

For more information, contact:
Greenhaven Press
27500 Drake Rd.
Farmington Hills, MI 48331-3535
Or you can visit our Internet site at gale.cengage.com

LIBRARY OF CONGRESS CATALOGING-IN-PUBLICATION DATA

The Arab Spring / Margaret Haerens and Lynn M. Zott, book editors.
    p. cm. -- (Opposing viewpoints)
    Includes bibliographical references and index.
    ISBN 978-0-7377-6042-2 (hardcover) -- ISBN 978-0-7377-6043-9 (pbk.)
    1. Arab countries--Politics and government--21st century. 2. Democratization--Arab countries--History--21st century. 3. Protest movements--Arab countries--History--21st century. I. Haerens, Margaret. II. Zott, Lynn M. (Lynn Marie), 1969-
    JQ1850.A91A75 2012
    909'.097492708312--dc23

2012007813

Printed in the United States of America
1 2 3 4 5 6 7 16 15 14 13 12

Contents

Chapter 3: How Should the United States Respond to the Arab Spring?

Why Consider Opposing Viewpoints?

> *"The only way in which a human being can make some approach to knowing the whole of a subject is by hearing what can be said about it by persons of every variety of opinion and studying all modes in which it can be looked at by every character of mind. No wise man ever acquired his wisdom in any mode but this."*
>
> *John Stuart Mill*

In our media-intensive culture it is not difficult to find differing opinions. Thousands of newspapers and magazines and dozens of radio and television talk shows resound with differing points of view. The difficulty lies in deciding which opinion to agree with and which "experts" seem the most credible. The more inundated we become with differing opinions and claims, the more essential it is to hone critical reading and thinking skills to evaluate these ideas. Opposing Viewpoints books address this problem directly by presenting stimulating debates that can be used to enhance and teach these skills. The varied opinions contained in each book examine many different aspects of a single issue. While examining these conveniently edited opposing views, readers can develop critical thinking skills such as the ability to compare and contrast authors' credibility, facts, argumentation styles, use of persuasive techniques, and other stylistic tools. In short, the Opposing Viewpoints Series is an ideal way to attain the higher-level thinking and reading skills so essential in a culture of diverse and contradictory opinions.

In addition to providing a tool for critical thinking, Opposing Viewpoints books challenge readers to question their own strongly held opinions and assumptions. Most people form their opinions on the basis of upbringing, peer pressure, and personal, cultural, or professional bias. By reading carefully balanced opposing views, readers must directly confront new ideas as well as the opinions of those with whom they disagree. This is not to argue simplistically that everyone who reads opposing views will—or should—change his or her opinion. Instead, the series enhances readers' understanding of their own views by encouraging confrontation with opposing ideas. Careful examination of others' views can lead to the readers' understanding of the logical inconsistencies in their own opinions, perspective on why they hold an opinion, and the consideration of the possibility that their opinion requires further evaluation.

Evaluating Other Opinions

To ensure that this type of examination occurs, Opposing Viewpoints books present all types of opinions. Prominent spokespeople on different sides of each issue as well as well-known professionals from many disciplines challenge the reader. An additional goal of the series is to provide a forum for other, less known, or even unpopular viewpoints. The opinion of an ordinary person who has had to make the decision to cut off life support from a terminally ill relative, for example, may be just as valuable and provide just as much insight as a medical ethicist's professional opinion. The editors have two additional purposes in including these less known views. One, the editors encourage readers to respect others' opinions—even when not enhanced by professional credibility. It is only by reading or listening to and objectively evaluating others' ideas that one can determine whether they are worthy of consideration. Two, the inclusion of such viewpoints encourages the important critical thinking skill of objectively evaluating an author's credentials and bias. This evaluation will illuminate an author's reasons for taking a particular stance on an issue and will aid in readers' evaluation of the author's ideas.

It is our hope that these books will give readers a deeper understanding of the issues debated and an appreciation of the complexity of even seemingly simple issues when good and honest people disagree. This awareness is particularly important in a democratic society such as ours in which people enter into public debate to determine the common good. Those with whom one disagrees should not be regarded as enemies but rather as people whose views deserve careful examination and may shed light on one's own.

Thomas Jefferson once said that "difference of opinion leads to inquiry, and inquiry to truth." Jefferson, a broadly educated man, argued that "if a nation expects to be ignorant and free . . . it expects what never was and never will be." As individuals and as a nation, it is imperative that we consider the opinions of others and examine them with skill and discernment. The Opposing Viewpoints series is intended to help readers achieve this goal.

David L. Bender and Bruno Leone,
Founders

Introduction

> *"Sometimes, in the course of history, the actions of ordinary citizens spark movements for change because they speak to a longing for freedom that has built up for years."*
>
> —President Barack Obama

Introduction

On December 17, 2010, a twenty-six-year-old man, Mohamed Bouazizi, was on his way to work in the market in the town of Sidi Bouzid, Tunisia, where he worked every day selling fruit to support his mother and siblings. That morning he got into a confrontation with a local policewoman over the location of his cart, and she confiscated some of Bouazizi's fruit. Enraged, he went to the police station and demanded to get his confiscated fruit back. He was turned away. Bouazizi then went to the municipal headquarters and demanded to see the governor. Again, he was turned away. Bouazizi left, bought paint fuel, and returned to the street in front of the government building. He then poured the flammable liquid over his head and body and set himself on fire.

The story of what happened quickly spread through the streets of Sidi Bouzid. Many people identified immediately with Bouazizi's desperate rage at the constant humiliations perpetrated on regular citizens by the police and petty government officials. Reports surfaced that the police were corrupt and had harassed poor young men like Bouazizi constantly, preventing them from earning the money they needed to support their families. People believed that it was impossible to find justice in a system that was already stacked against them and that favored the wealthy and the well connected. For many Tunisians, life was full of the indignities and injustice that Bouazizi experienced on a daily basis. Some may have even felt so distressed and hopeless that they had also considered desperate measures. In a matter of hours, the legend of Bouazizi's shocking act spread throughout the town. He became a martyr to a community sick and tired of being abused, exploited, and oppressed. The people turned against what they saw as the reason for his extreme actions: the government.

Crowds quickly gathered outside of the government offices and chanted slogans, demanding justice for Bouazizi and reforms to address the rampant corruption and injustice of the Tunisian government led by the dictator Zine El Abidine Ben Ali. The next day, police were sent to break up the protests. Violence erupted, and two protesters were killed. Protests spread to nearby Kasserine, Thala, and other towns. In the capital, Tunis, large crowds organized in front of the prime minister's residence in Kasbah Square to make their voices heard on a number of issues: government corruption, income inequality, rising unemployment, lack of economic opportunity, and restrictions to free speech. Tunisian people from all walks of life joined in the protests, which got larger and engulfed the entire country. On January 14, 2011, Zine El Abidine Ben Ali fled to Saudi Arabia. The people had won.

Activists in other Arab countries were inspired by the successful Tunisian protests. In Egypt, protesters planned a national day of revolt on January 25, 2011. The date was chosen to coincide with National Police Day, and the main complaint was about police brutality under the rule of Egypt's dictator, Hosni Mubarak. On that day, mass demonstrations were called in cities all over Egypt to protest police and government corruption. The next day, the government shut down the Internet for most of the country, hoping to cut off the ability of protesters to organize more mass demonstrations. On January 28, Mubarak gave a speech and pledged to form a new government that would address some of the protester's concerns. After protests grew and reports of clashes between demonstrators and security forces were published, Mubarak promised to step down from office after his current term and enact significant political reforms. However, violence escalated in Tahrir Square and elsewhere as protesters refused to back down and be placated by Mubarak's promises. Nothing less than the Egyptian president's immediate resignation would suffice. On February 11, it was announced that Mubarak had resigned and leadership of the country was assumed by Egypt's Supreme Council of the Armed Forces.

The Arab Spring also made its way to Libya, where protesters called for the ouster of its dictatorial leader, Muammar Gaddafi. On February 17, 2011, the uprising began in the city of Benghazi and quickly spread to the nation's capital, Tripoli. Like in Tunisia and Egypt, demonstrators called for an end to government corruption, police brutality, lack of economic opportunity, cronyism, and severe restrictions on speech and freedom of expression. Gaddafi responded to the protests with brutal violence, as government security forces and foreign mercenaries beat and shot demonstrators. As the violence escalated, an opposition army was formed to forcibly overthrow the regime. If Gaddafi got the upper hand, international observers speculated that he would mercilessly slaughter thousands of protesters and opposition fighters.

Because of those concerns, the international community decided to intervene. On March 17, 2011, the United Nations Security Council adopted Resolution 1973, which called for immediate intervention in the conflict. The North Atlantic Treaty Organization (NATO) established a no-fly zone over much of Libya and provided air strikes against Gaddafi forces. In late August, rebel troops gained control over Tripoli, and Gaddafi and his family went into hiding. His reign in Libya was over. On October 20, 2011, Gaddafi was caught hiding near his hometown of Sirte, where he was killed by rebel forces.

The Arab Spring has spread to other countries as well. Protesters in Syria have called for the resignation of President Bashar al-Assad. Thousands of Yemenis have taken to the streets to demand the ouster of President Abdullah Saleh. In Bahrain, demonstrators demanded greater political freedom and respect for human rights under the regime of King Hamad bin Isa Al Khalifa. There have also been significant protest movements in Algeria, Iraq, the Golan Heights, Jordan, Morocco, and Oman. Some of these protest movements were productive and led to political reform. Others resulted in crackdowns from government security forces and further political repression. Many of them are ongoing, as the issues that sparked them remain.

The authors of the viewpoints in *Opposing Viewpoints: The Arab Spring* explore consequences of the Arab Spring in the following chapters: What Caused the Arab Spring?, How Should the International Community Respond to the Arab Spring?, How Should the United States Respond to the Arab Spring?, and What Are the Social and Political Effects of the Arab Spring? The information in this volume provides insight into the conditions that inspired the protests, the reaction of the international community and specifically the United States, and what the Arab Spring may mean to certain groups and communities around the world.

What Caused the Arab Spring?

Chapter Preface

As the Arab Spring began to spread across the Middle East and North Africa at the end of 2010, the rest of the world watched transfixed as ordinary people mobilized in large numbers and bravely protested in the streets, often risking harm and even death from cruel state security forces. In some cases, such as Tunisia and Egypt, governments toppled. In others, like Libya, the corrupt regime was pushed by international forces and finished off by Libyan opposition troops. Further unrest continues to threaten regimes in Syria, Yemen, and Bahrain. The quest for self-determination, economic justice, and democratic governance was sweeping a region once characterized by corrupt, autocratic, and often brutally repressive leaders.

To see the Arab Spring gather momentum after years of oppression and harsh treatment was inspiring to many. For many pundits and scholars, the question invariably asked was "why now?" Why did this movement succeed when so many other attempts at democratic reform fail? After all, Hosni Mubarak reigned in Egypt for thirty years. In Libya, Muammar Gaddafi ruled with an iron fist for forty-two years. Tunisia's ousted leader, Zine El Abidine Ben Ali, was the leader of Tunisia for twenty-four years. These were leaders who had spent years eliminating dissidents and the opposition, installing cronies in every part of government, and instituting policies that reinforced their influence and control in every part of their bureaucratic system. Yet, from the outside, it looked as if all that entrenched power was swept away in mere months by people ready to take back the reins and institute a more fair, democratic government system.

As in other successful uprisings, there is not just one simple reason why the spark of discontent fans into flames of revolution. Movements like the Arab Spring arise from a number of interrelated political, economic, and social reasons. Some of them are pure and at the heart of what every human being wants: economic and social justice; access to education and jobs; a real sense of self-determination; and a government that does not harass, repress, or humiliate the individual because of economic status, religion, or ethnicity. Others may be political in nature, such as a philosophical opposition to authoritarianism and a desire for democratic reform. In some cases, individuals or groups may want to overthrow a government to take power themselves, install their cronies in government positions, and reap the economic benefits. In the case of the Arab Spring, many commentators were concerned that some protesters wanted to install Islamist regimes that would impose draconian Islamic laws that would threaten the rights of women and religious minorities and oppose American foreign policy goals. In the worst case, American officials feared that terrorist groups would gain power in these countries and pursue violence against Western countries.

Another much-discussed reason for the Arab Spring was the rise of information technology, especially social media. Commentators contend that it is technology that facilitated the widespread collective action that inspired ordinary citizens to protest and act early on, when it seemed futile and extremely dangerous to stand up against a powerful government force. Early protesters used their cell phones to film government brutality and posted the videos on YouTube and other sites on the Internet, allowing other citizens to see events right after they happened and also subverted the government's efforts to downplay resistance and stifle the truth about what was really happening on the streets. Twitter alerted citizens to protests that were happening in real time and warned people about military strikes, snipers, and dangerous areas to avoid. Facebook was also used to disseminate information about government atrocities and marshal support against the regime.

One well-known example of the power of social media in the Arab Spring is the case of Khaled Mohamed Saeed, a young Egyptian protester who was killed under mysterious circumstances during the uprising in June 2010. A Facebook page, entitled "We Are All Khaled Said," posted pictures of his disfigured corpse and spread allegations that he had been beaten to death by Egyptian security forces after being arrested during a protest. Thousands of people all over the world viewed the page and posted their support of Khaled and the protesters. Khaled Mohamed Saeed came to symbolize the deadly repressive violence of the Mubarak regime and to reinforce why so many ordinary people in Egypt were joining the opposition movement.

The role of social media is one of the topics explored in the following chapter, which examines the reasons behind the revolutionary movement. Other viewpoints in the chapter include the effects of globalization, education, and corruption on the uprisings in the Arab world.

> *"Hundreds of millions of Arabs feel they have been denied both their human rights and their citizenship rights, the result of decades of socioeconomic stresses and political deprivations."*

The Arab Spring Was Triggered by a Desire for Democracy and Social Justice

Rami G. Khouri

Rami G. Khouri is editor at large of the Daily Star *in Beirut, Lebanon, and the director of the Issam Fares Institute for Public Policy and International Affairs. In the following viewpoint, he contends that the Arab Spring was ignited by the desire for a legitimate governing system and an end to the humiliation that people have suffered under the tyranny and corruption of their rulers. Khouri argues that the Arab people are demanding a governing system that is accountable to the needs of its citizens, including minorities. Also, there is a burning desire for a government that believes in social justice and equal opportunity, as well as reflects the values of its citizens.*

As you read, consider the following questions:

1. What Arab countries does the author cite as not partici-
   pating in the Arab Spring?

2. According to a 2009 Gallup poll, what percentage of
   Arab youths feel they can find good, affordable housing?

3. What country does the author say is the region-wide
   test case for the Arab Spring?

When Mohamed Bouazizi set himself on fire in rural Tunisia on December 17, 2010, he set in motion a dynamic that goes far beyond the overthrow of individual dictators. We are witnessing nothing less than the awakening,
throughout the Arab world, of several phenomena that are
critical for stable statehood: the citizen, the citizenry, legitimacy of authority, a commitment to social justice, genuine
politics, national self-determination and, ultimately, true sovereignty. It took hundreds of years for the United States and
Western Europe to develop governance and civil society systems that affirmed those principles, even if incompletely or er-
ratically, so we should be realistic in our expectations of how
long it will take Arab societies to do so.

The countries where citizens are more actively agitating or
fighting for their rights—Libya, Tunisia, Egypt, Syria, Bahrain
and Yemen are the most advanced to date—have very different local conditions and forms of governance, with ruling
elites displaying a wide range of legitimacy in the eyes of their
people. Governments have responded to the challenge in a variety of ways, from the flight of the Tunisian and Egyptian
leaderships to violent military repression in Syria, Libya and
Bahrain, to the attempt to negotiate limited constitutional
transformations in Jordan, Morocco and Oman. A few countries that have not experienced major demonstrations—Algeria and Sudan are the most significant—are likely to experience domestic effervescence in due course. Only the handful

of wealthy oil producers (like Saudi Arabia, Kuwait, Qatar and the United Arab Emirates) seem largely exempt, for now, from this wave of citizen demands.

The Reasons for the Arab Spring

Two words capture every important dimension of the Arab awakening: "humiliation" and "legitimacy." They explain why the Arab region is erupting, and what needs to be done to satisfy popular demands. The typical Arab citizen, with few exceptions, has felt humiliated in recent decades by his or her government. Hundreds of millions of Arabs feel they have been denied both their human rights and their citizenship rights, the result of decades of socioeconomic stresses and political deprivations. These include petty and large-scale corruption; police brutality; abuse of power; favoritism; unemployment; poor wages; unequal opportunities; inefficient or nonexistent public services; lack of freedom of expression and association; state control of media, culture and education; and many other dimensions of the modern Arab security state. At the same time, ordinary men and women in countries across the region have seen small groups of families in the ruling elite grow fabulously rich simply because of their connections.

Young people sparked the revolt because they are generally the ones who suffer the most grievous consequences of the failed political order. They are unable to enjoy life's full opportunities and rewards, in terms of education, work, income and material well-being. Millions of young Arabs took to the streets this year [2011] because they refused to acquiesce in either the legacy of stunted citizenship or the prospect of limited life opportunities. Their increasingly mediocre and irrelevant educations meant they had difficulty finding jobs that pay enough to live decently, get married and start a family. They saw in front of them an entire lifetime of restricted opportunities and stolen rights. When they tried to speak out against unfair and corrupt practices, they were prevented from doing so by police and security agencies.

Polling Data

Considerable polling data are now available to confirm this condition. The Gallup organization and Silatech in Doha, Qatar, have polled Arabs between the ages of 15 and 29 throughout the Middle East and North Africa, providing unprecedented insight into two important backdrops to the revolt: Young people are strongly dissatisfied with their national conditions and personal prospects, and the concerns and fears of young Arabs are shared by adults across the region. Where significant differences occur, they reflect primarily the gap between largely satisfied youth in the few wealthy oil-producing countries, and vulnerable and fearful youth who are the vast majority of the region's 350 million people. The 2009 data show, for example, that Arab men and women between 15 and 29 have a strong desire to migrate permanently in quest of a job and a better life; but this desire is very uneven. It reaches 40–45 percent in some countries, like Yemen, Morocco and Tunisia, but doesn't eclipse 7 percent in the Gulf states. Just over half of Arab youth (55 percent) have confidence in their government (in poorer Arab societies it's as low as 37 percent, while in oil-producing Qatar it's 90 percent). Only 45 percent of Arab youth have confidence in their mass media, and even fewer (around 34 percent) believe their national elections are honest. Just 32 percent of young people feel they can find good, affordable housing, which routinely delays plans to marry and start a family.

The lives of many young Arabs follow a trajectory of sentiments that starts with irritation and inconvenience; grows to anger, vulnerability and resentment; and finally reaches desperation and degradation. Treated as something less than human by their governments, barely able to make a living and enduring the added pain caused by decades of invading foreign armies and, in the case of Palestine, Syria and Lebanon, Israeli colonizers and siege masters, they have endured humiliations so severe that they can no longer endure it in silence or acquiescence.

Creating a Legitimate Governing System

The revolt we are witnessing is not about ideology. It is mostly about men and women who, so brutalized by their own and foreign powers, are asserting their fundamental humanity— their right to use all their human faculties; to read, speak, listen, think, debate, create and enjoy to the full extent of their God-given ability or desire, whether in culture, politics, art, media, technology or any other arena.

The structural political antidote to humiliation is legitimacy: a governing system that is anchored in the consent of the governed and is accountable to the needs, rights and aspirations of citizens. Public institutions and decisions should reflect the will of the majority while protecting the rights of minorities. The two most critical elements of legitimate governance systems in Arab-Islamic lands are accountability and a sense of justice, or equity. Constitutions, parliaments, electoral laws and other mechanisms can be devised in many forms—tinged with Arabism, Islamism, tribalism, cosmopolitanism—but above all, they must be legitimate in the eyes of their people if the societies are finally to emerge from the dark tunnel of the security state and its stultifying, corrupting legacy. Legitimacy opens the door to normalcy in politics and daily life.

The citizen with rights—the most basic element of legitimate statehood—is the first building block of the Arab awakening. Mohamed Bouazizi inspired the mass protests that have planted the seeds for stable citizenship across the region—the spontaneous action of a single indignant and dehumanized person resonated widely and powerfully with millions of his compatriots. By sparking mass resistance and national transformation through his refusal to live in humiliation, he should be seen in the same light as a line of historic figures around the world whose self-sacrifice transformed their societies— Rosa Parks, Lech Walesa, Steve Biko, Václav Havel, Nelson Mandela, Andrei Sakharov, Aung San Suu Kyi—because millions of their countrymen and women shared the same goals.

The Role of Accountability

When hundreds of thousands of Egyptians took to the streets in January and February to remove the [President Hosni] Mubarak regime, they tasted their first dose not only of individual empowerment but also of collective citizenship rights. When they returned to the streets in July, they reaffirmed their insistence on transforming their government so that it was more legitimate in their eyes, and reflected the two critical elements they felt were missing from the old system: accountability and social justice.

Egyptians and Tunisians, and all Arabs, as we will soon learn, do not want to see their fellow countrymen and women killed by the hundreds without anyone being held accountable. This is what Arab regimes have routinely done; it is also what Israel has done in Palestine and Lebanon, and what the United States and other foreign armies did in Iraq in recent years. It is not surprising that these three—the corrupt Arab regimes, Israel and the United States—are the main targets of anger and indignity, because a central message of the Arab awakening is that there should be no abuse of power or killing with impunity (only the domestic dimension of these sentiments is operational, with foreign policy issues to follow in due course). Behind this emphasis on accountability lurks an equally important concept that is central to the spirit of the awakening: social justice, the critical but underappreciated philosophical underpinning of the new Arab citizenry.

The Role of Dignity in the Arab Spring

The term "dignity" involves a dual demand: first, for the dignity of the individual in the face of rulers who treat their subjects as without rights and beneath contempt. But there is also a demand for the collective dignity of proud states like Egypt, and of the Arabs as a people. This was the demand that nationalist leaders rode to power starting in the 1950s, as they targeted colonialism and neocolonialism.

Rashid Khalidi, "The Arab Spring,"
Nation, *March 21, 2011.*

Social Justice

Social justice is about removing structures that abuse and subjugate citizens and turn them into powerless victims of oligarchies and autocracies. It is about ensuring that public authorities reflect the values, and serve the needs and rights, of citizens. Egypt leads the way in this important new dynamic, in which millions of individuals have come together to demand that the authorities rule with the consent of the governed. In the Egyptian case, the citizenry is insisting that the transitional authority, the Supreme Council of the Armed Forces, carry out the key demands of the January revolution. For the first time, public opinion matters in some Arab countries.

The new Egyptian regime swiftly assuaged some grievances through moves to arrest, investigate and try former officials; dissolve parliament and outlaw Mubarak's National Democratic Party; and suspend the constitution and write a new one subject to public approval. The beginning, in early

August [2011], of the trial of Mubarak, his sons and former officials was a powerful turning point in the Egyptian and Arab political psyche, because it reaffirmed the ordinary citizen's trust in a system that held power accountable and put in the dock officials accused of abusing, robbing or killing fellow citizens. Less rapid progress has been made, though, on lifting the state of emergency; protecting protesters and holding police accountable for killing demonstrators; reforming the security forces; limiting executive authority; fighting corruption; and improving economic conditions for ordinary Egyptians. These issues resonate widely across the Arab world. How governments respond to them will determine whether societies make a smooth transition to democracy or street confrontations persist for some time.

The Birth of Politics

Even as demands grow for these three building blocks of credible governance—the basic rights of the citizen and citizenry, and a legitimate state authority that is accountable to the people's demand for social justice—we are witnessing the fourth element in the Arab awakening: the birth of politics. In Tunisia and Egypt, citizens are directly contesting for power by forming groups that engage politically with other groups to define new state norms and policies. These include civil society organizations, religious movements, political parties, the private sector, military authorities, youth groups, labor movements, women's organizations and many others. As this contest for and over power develops through a combination of means—parliamentary, electoral, judicial and media actions, as well as peaceful street demonstrations—it midwifes the birth of pluralistic, citizen-based politics. This contrasts sharply with the legacy of Arab decision making, monopolized by ruling families and elites who depended heavily on foreign powers for their survival.

In countries where regimes have not been changed or descended into violent confrontations, citizens have in many cases forced the governments to engage them in dialogue aimed at reforming or reconfiguring the constitutional systems. If the changes that emanate from such discussions are deemed superficial, citizens will no doubt return to the streets to demand real change, as we have witnessed already in several countries.

These developments point to the ultimate issues at stake in the Arab revolts, the prize, if you will: national sovereignty and self-determination. The contest over sovereignty has been at the heart of the confrontation between citizens and ruling authorities since December, but it dates back decades. It is about who holds ultimate power, who is in charge of decision making in the nominally independent Arab countries. Most national decisions in Arab countries for much of the past century have been made by small groups of unelected men who dominate the political elite with their security services. A widely shared public sentiment across the region is that Arab ruling elites have responded more to the dictates of foreign powers than to their own people. When decisions have been made internally, they have primarily carried out the interests of the ruling families and their cronies, or the security and military systems that were the ultimate powers. Nowhere in national decision making did ordinary Arab citizens feel that their voices were heard, or that their rights and sentiments mattered.

An Audacious Quest

Egypt is once again the region-wide test case of what happens at this delicate and probably decisive transitional moment. The demonstrators who returned to Tahrir Square and other city centers across the country in June and July, before suspending their protests for the holy month of Ramadan in August—and those who continue to take to the streets in Syria,

Libya, Bahrain and Yemen—want to make power answerable to the will of the citizenry. Through the instrument of citizen sovereignty, Arabs are struggling to shed the ugly and embarrassing legacy of modern statehood, in which they enjoyed independence without real self-determination and citizens for the most part never had an opportunity to define national values, governance systems, ideologies or policies.

The Arab awakening is in the first stages of creating a citizen-based sovereignty that values social justice and equal opportunity. It is an audacious quest, for Mohamed Bouazizi and the millions of Arabs inspired by him, just as it was for Rosa Parks and the civil rights movement in the American South.

> "What is happening in the Middle East
> does not fit into the simplistic liberal
> democratic narrative [also known as
> the] Arab Spring, in the same way that
> events in the region during the Cold
> War could not be explained based on
> the old Communist story line."

The Arab Spring Is More of a Power Grab than a Democratic Awakening

Leon T. Hadar

*Leon T. Hadar is an author and research fellow at the Cato In-
stitute. In the following viewpoint, he maintains that the uprising known as the Arab Spring is motivated not by a desire for
social justice or democracy, but by the desire for power. Hadar
asserts that the Western media have a distorted view of the situation and are perpetuating misinformation on the reasons behind and goals of the Arab Spring. He concludes that Islamist
forces are behind the protests, as they are looking to overturn
secularist governments and gain power for themselves.*

As you read, consider the following questions:

1. According to the author, what did the Soviet newspaper *Pravda* say about the upheaval in the Middle East in the 1950s, 1960s, and 1970s?

2. What positive things does the author say Hosni Mubarak and Zine El Abidine Ben Ali did for their countries?

3. What does the author say is the main conflict in Bahrain?

Skim through old editorials that were published in the Soviet Communist Party's *Pravda* newspaper during the Cold War and you'll have a lot of fun, laughing out loud when reading about all those loopy notions that the people in Moscow held about the upheaval taking place in the Middle East at the time. Historians of the Middle East explain that the region was then going through major structural, political and economic changes resulting from, among other things, the collapse of the British and French empires, the 1948 Arab-Israeli War, the impact of secular Arab nationalism and socialism, the rise of military elites, and various religious, ethnic and tribal conflicts.

But according to the old *Pravda* and the Soviet officials who published it, things were actually very simple. Whether it was the military coup in Egypt (1952), the periodic unrest in Syria and Iraq in the 1950s, or the civil war in Yemen in the 1960s, the Communist narrative of the day saw these and the other crises taking place in the region as the outcome of the grand struggle between the ruling 'feudal elites' backed by 'international capitalism' and the freedom-loving representatives of 'the proletariat'.

And it was not surprising, of course, that the Soviets were supposed to be on the side of the courageous members of the working class while the Americans were supporting the corrupt Arab monarchs and sheiks.

History Repeats Itself

One wonders if 50 years from now, when researchers scan through old issues of the *Washington Post* and analyse its coverage of the current upheaval in the Arab Middle East they are going to chuckle as they try to figure out what those American pundits were smoking when they kept insisting that this year's [2011's] military coup in Egypt, the political unrest in Syria and Iraq, and the civil war in Yemen (and in Libya and Bahrain) were all a manifestation of an inexorable drive toward freedom and liberal democracy, including freedom of religion and women's rights. These events are a replay of sorts of the kind of changes that took place in Eastern Europe in 1989.

In reality, the so-called Arab Spring consists of a mishmash of antigovernment demonstrations triggered in most cases by police overreaction and fuelled by economic hard times (Tunisia and Egypt), ethnic and religious tensions (Syria and Bahrain) and tribal rivalries (Libya and Yemen) as well as by growing public perception that the global hegemon—the United States—that was helping keep ruling regimes in place is losing its power.

The Reality of the Middle East Situation

So, while no one denies that Hosni Mubarak in Egypt and Zine El Abidine Ben Ali in Tunisia were ruthless autocrats engaged in human rights violations, the two were also responsible for liberalising their socialist economies and opening their countries to Western investment while resisting the Islamist push to restrict the rights of women and religious minorities.

And there is no doubt that even under the best case scenario, the elections scheduled to take place in Egypt and Tunisia are going to strengthen the power of the Islamist parties. This, in turn, is bound to exacerbate tensions between Muslims and Christian Copts [a Christian religious group] in Egypt and increase the influence of religion in these two countries and pose a risk to secular women and men.

In addition, the economic liberalisation that has taken place in Egypt and Tunisia in recent years is being threatened by demands, supported by some of the new political forces, to increase government control of parts of the economy. They want this done to improve the condition of the economically distressed middle class and poor.

A Struggle for Power

At the same time, the tribal warfare in Yemen and Libya and the sectarian tensions in Syria (between the ruling minority Alawites [a branch of Shia Islam] and the Sunni majority) and in Bahrain (between the ruling minority Sunnis and the Shiite majority) have less to do with promoting the cause of liberal democracy and more with the struggle for power between identity groups, not unlike what is taking place in Iraq (between Shiites, Sunnis and Kurds [the Kurdish people]).

The Sunnis in Bahrain (backed by the Saudi theocracy) discriminate against the Shiite majority (supported by the Iranian theocracy) as they maintain what is the freest economy in the region, while the ruling Alawites in Syria are strongly committed to secular principles as they repress the Sunni majority and enjoy close ties to the Iranian theocracy. And so it goes.

In short, what is happening in the Middle East does not fit into the simplistic liberal democratic narrative [also known as the] Arab Spring, in the same way that events in the region during the Cold War could not be explained based on the old Communist story line. And like the case of Moscow at the time, the ability of the US to shape the events in the Middle East is limited. Perhaps the time has come for the people of the region to start writing their own narratives. It might get ugly and end up being not the kind of narrative that Americans like. But it will still be their own narrative.

VIEWPOINT3

| "These really are 'Facebook'—Internet,
mobile phone, social networking—
revolutions."

Social Media Ignited
the Arab Spring

Johnny West

Johnny West is the author of Karama!: Journeys Through the
Arab Spring. *In the following viewpoint, he assesses the key role
of social media and the Internet in the Arab Spring. West asserts
that social media had a bigger role than just coordinating protests or events; in fact, he maintains, it functioned to provide access to "a whole new universe of information" for disgruntled
and angry citizens. Further, West asserts, it allowed regular
people to find out that there were more people out there who felt
the same way and were willing to take steps to challenge the status quo.*

As you read, consider the following questions:

1. According to West, what do critics think about the Facebook revolution?

Ed Stein. Reprinted with permission.

2. What percentage of the population in Libya could access the Internet by 2008, according to the author?

3. Who is Satoor, according to the viewpoint?

Sometimes hype is justified. Earlier this year [2011], the airwaves and opinion columns of media around the world were full of talk of Facebook revolution in the Arab Spring, how social networking had shaped a new political era in the Middle East, shaking down a geopolitical balance of Arab autocracy that had existed for decades.

Then came the response from the heavyweights, commentators, academics, Middle East specialists: "Facebook Revolution" is naïve, propagated by cyber-utopians who don't understand that the rest of the world doesn't have broadband and that the revolutions in Egypt, Tunisia and elsewhere are about long-standing and complex issues like mass unemployment, crony capitalism and the stifling nature of dictatorship, albeit dressed with a veneer of liberalism and, in some cases, backed by strategic alliances with Western countries. . . .

The Facebook Revolutions

But, after a few months kicking around the revolutions, hanging around in the small towns and back streets of North Africa and speaking to everyone you could imagine, I've come to the conclusion that the original hype is correct. These really are "Facebook"—Internet, mobile phone, social networking—revolutions.

They simply would not have happened without digital technologies. And what's more, it's only just beginning.

Those who would paint a limited role for the Internet and digital technologies tend to make two mistakes:

- First, they see information in a clinical sense, simply what it conveys that wasn't already known, or its immediate and short-term impact on action, its ability to move cogs and wheels.

- Second, although they accuse geeks of being naïve in giving too much importance to technology, they themselves in fact project the "Western" model of nuclear-individual-on-laptop onto social structures which don't work that way with anything, let alone expensive technology.

Opening the Door to a New World

'I honestly think WikiLeaks had something to do with our revolution. It's not that people didn't know the facts already. But now it was in front of us, in our faces. We knew that the Americans knew. And we knew that they didn't think a lot of [Tunisian president Zine El Abidine] Ben Ali, whatever they said in public . . . Humiliation. It had become humiliating to have a president like Ben Ali.'

—*Nabil, a professor at Kairawan University*

39

The Internet's role in social protest does not begin, and is not limited to During-the-Revolution, "the demo will take place at this spot at 3:30 on Tuesday afternoon." A society's exposure to a whole new universe of information—and by society we simply mean enough influential individuals in it, not a universality, or some flat percentage which ignores the kind of "social networking" people did long before Mark Zuckerberg was even born: around the kitchen table, at the bus stop, at your cousin's wedding—sooner or later affects their self-identity, their aspirations and sense of place in the world.

Finding Solidarity in Social Media

This is what happened in the Arab Spring. Hundreds of thousands of bloggers, and through them tens of millions of their fellow citizens, experienced a great big Before-the-Revolution of personal expression—'This regime stinks and I have to tell the world'; solidarity—'Oh my God you feel that way too!'; even embarrassment—'Gosh, it seems like everyone thinks the Big Man is rubbish.'

In Libya, when the Internet started to reach two or three percent of the population in 2007 and 2008, so did Satoor, a cartoonist whose parodies of [Libyan ruler Muammar] Gaddafi made him an object of mockery. Satoor's cartoons were printed out, and imitated, in the towns of the east—Tobruk, Bayda and Benghazi—hours after the rebels took them from Gaddafi's forces. Clearly the ideas had been there for some time.

Once you have the Internet, it's like a big *Psst* in your ear. However serious the oppression and your very real fear of the regime, you can never actually believe them again, and you know it's the same for nearly everyone else. Gradually, it becomes hard even to pretend to believe them.

So what about now, in After-the-Revolution Egypt and Tunisia, and maybe other countries to come? Some interesting things are afoot.

> *"Those who believe that these [activist] networks were purely virtual and spontaneous are ignorant of the recent history of cyber-activism in the Middle East—to say nothing of the support that it's received . . . from Western governments, foundations and corporations."*

Social Media Did Not Cause the Arab Spring

Evgeny Morozov

Evgeny Morozov is an author, a fellow at the New America Foundation, and contributing editor of Foreign Policy *and* Boston Review. *In the following viewpoint, he counters the prevailing view that social media was the driving force behind the Arab Spring. Morozov contends that history will show that the movement did not pop up spontaneously on the Internet and spread because of social media, but rather it is based in grassroots activism with leaders supported for years by Western governments, foundations, and corporations. He argues that the current fascination with the role of social media and the Internet in the Arab revolutions will eventually subside.*

As you read, consider the following questions:

1. What argument does the author make in his book, *The Net Delusion*, about the role of social media?

2. Does the author agree with Timothy Garton Ash's theory that all the revolutions are "telerevolutions"?

3. Why does the author believe that social media companies are overestimating their own importance in the Arab Spring?

Tweets were sent. Dictators were toppled. Internet = democracy. QED [abbreviation of the Latin phrase *quod erat demonstrandum*, meaning "that which was demonstrated"].

Sadly, this is the level of nuance in most popular accounts of the Internet's contribution to the recent unrest in the Middle East.

It's been extremely entertaining to watch cyber-utopians—adherents of the view that digital tools of social networking such as Facebook and Twitter can summon up social revolutions out of the ether—trip over one another in an effort to put another nail in the coffin of cyber-realism, the position I've recently advanced in my book *The Net Delusion*. In my book, I argue that these digital tools are simply, well, tools, and social change continues to involve many painstaking, longer-term efforts to engage with political institutions and reform movements.

Since the Internet's cheerleaders can't bury cyber-realism any more than they can secede from history, they've had to design their own straw-man interpretation of the cyber-realist position, equating it with a view that the Internet doesn't matter. This is a caricature of the cyber-realist worldview that doesn't really square with parts of my book that very explicitly state—here is just one quote—that "the Internet is more important and disruptive than [its greatest advocates] have previously theorised".

The Case of Malcolm Gladwell

Or take the ongoing persecution of Malcolm Gladwell, who is increasingly painted as some kind of a neo-Luddite [an individual who opposes modern technology]. In an online chat that Gladwell did for the *New Yorker*'s website shortly after his infamous attack on the notion of "Twitter Revolution" was published last October [in 2010], he explicitly stated (no less than three times) that the Internet can be an effective tool for political change when used by grassroots organisations (as opposed to atomised individuals). Thus, simply showing that the Internet was used to publicise, and even organise, protests in the Middle East does nothing to counter his argument (which, by the way, I do not entirely endorse). To refute it, cyber-utopians would need to establish that there was no coordination of these protests by networks of grassroots activists—with leaders and hierarchies—who have forged strong ties (online or off-line or both) prior to the protests.

The Limited Role of Technology

What we have seen so far suggests otherwise. True, the principal organisers of Egypt's Facebook movement may not be revolutionary leaders in the conventional understanding of the term. (And how could they be, given the grim track record that former president Hosni Mubarak compiled—with Washington's complicity—in dispatching such leaders?) However, they did exercise leadership and acted strategically—even going into hiding a few days before the actual protests—just as leaders of a revolutionary cell would.

The collaborations between Tunisian and Egyptian cyber-activists—so widely celebrated in the press—were not virtual, either. In the space of a week in May 2009, I crashed two (independently organised) workshops in Cairo, where bloggers, techies, and activists from both countries were present in person, sharing tips on how to engage in advocacy and circumvent censorship; one of the attendees was the Tunisian

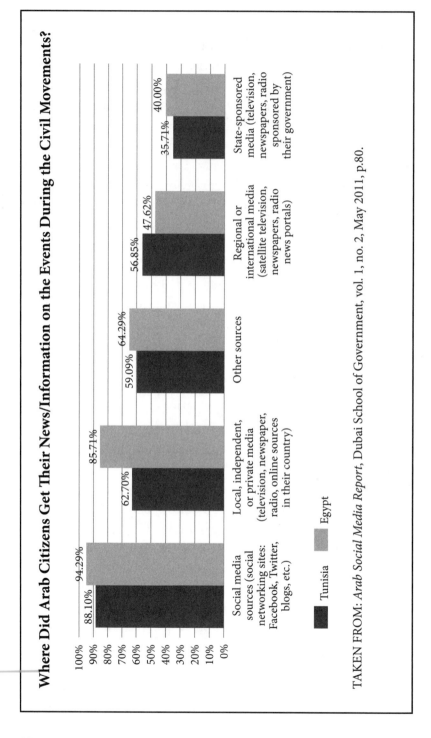

Where Did Arab Citizens Get Their News/Information on the Events During the Civil Movements?

TAKEN FROM: *Arab Social Media Report*, Dubai School of Government, vol. 1, no. 2, May 2011, p.80.

blogger Slim Amamou, who went on to become Tunisia's minister of sport and youth. One of these events was funded by the US government and the other by George Soros's Open Society Foundations (with which I'm affiliated).

The True Way the Arab Spring Developed

There were many more events like this—not just in Cairo, but also in Beirut and Dubai. Most of them were never publicised, since the security of many participants was at risk, but they effectively belie the idea that the recent protests were organised by random people doing random things online. Those who believe that these networks were purely virtual and spontaneous are ignorant of the recent history of cyber-activism in the Middle East—to say nothing of the support that it's received, sometimes successful but most often not, from Western governments, foundations and corporations. In September 2010, to take just one recent example, Google brought a dozen bloggers from the region to the freedom of expression conference the company convened in Budapest.

Tracing the evolution of these activist networks would require more than just studying their Facebook profiles; it would demand painstaking investigative work—on the phone and in the archives—that cannot happen overnight. One reason we keep talking about the role of Twitter and Facebook is that the immediate aftermath of the Middle Eastern spring has left us so little else to talk about; thoroughgoing political analysis of the causes of these revolutions won't be available for a few years.

Look Past the Technology

This points us to the real reason why so many cyber-utopians got angry with Gladwell: In a follow-up blog post to his article that appeared as the crowds were still occupying Tahrir Square [in Cairo, Egypt], he dared to suggest that the grievances that pushed protesters into the streets deserve far more attention than the tools by which they chose to organise. This was akin to spitting in the faces of the digerati—or, perhaps worse still, on their iPads—and they reacted accordingly.

And yet Gladwell was probably right: Today, the role of the telegraph in the 1917 Bolshevik revolution—just like the role of the tape recorder in the 1979 Iranian revolution and of the fax machine in the 1989 revolutions—is of interest to a handful of academics and virtually no one else. The fetishism of technology is at its strongest immediately after a revolution but tends to subside shortly afterward.

In his 1993 best seller, *The Magic Lantern*, Timothy Garton Ash, one of the most acute observers of the 1989 revolutions, proclaimed that "in Europe at the end of the 20th century, all revolutions are telerevolutions"—but in retrospect, the role of television in those events seems like a very minor point.

Will history consign Twitter and Facebook to much the same fate 20 years down the road? In all likelihood, yes. The current fascination with technology-driven accounts of political change in the Middle East is likely to subside, for a number of reasons.

The Importance of Human Agency

First of all, while the recent round of uprisings may seem spontaneous to Western observers—and therefore as magically disruptive as a rush-hour flash mob in San Francisco—the actual history of popular regime change tends to diminish the central role commonly ascribed to technology. By emphasising the liberating role of the tools and downplaying the role of human agency, such accounts make Americans feel proud of their own contribution to events in the Middle East. After all, the argument goes, such a spontaneous uprising wouldn't have succeeded before Facebook was around—so Silicon Valley deserves a lion's share of the credit. If, of course, the uprising was not spontaneous and its leaders chose Facebook simply because that's where everybody is, it's a far less glamorous story.

An Exaggeration of Social Media's Role

Second, social media—by the very virtue of being "social"—lends itself to glib, pundit-style overestimations of its own importance. In 1989, the fax machine industry didn't employ an army of lobbyists—and fax users didn't feel the same level of attachment to these clunky machines as today's Facebook users feel toward their all-powerful social network. Perhaps the outsize revolutionary claims for social media now circulating throughout the West are only a manifestation of Western guilt for wasting so much time on social media: After all, if it helps to spread democracy in the Middle East, it can't be all that bad to while away the hours "poking" your friends and playing FarmVille. But the recent history of technology strongly suggests that today's vogue for Facebook and Twitter will fade as online audiences migrate to new services. Already, tech enthusiasts are blushing at the memory of the serious academic conferences once devoted to the MySpace revolution.

Passions Are Running High

Third, the people who serve as our immediate sources about the protests may simply be too excited to provide a balanced view. Could it be that the Google sales executive Wael Ghonim—probably the first revolutionary with an MBA—who has emerged as the public face of Egypt's uprising, vowing to publish his own book about "Revolution 2.0," is slightly overstating the role of technology, while also downplaying his own role in the lead-up to the protests? After all, the world has yet to meet a Soviet dissident who doesn't think it was the fax machine that toppled the Politburo—or a former employee of Radio Free Europe or Voice of America who doesn't think it was Western radio broadcasting that brought down the Berlin Wall.

This is not to suggest that neither of these communications devices played a role in these decades-old uprisings—but it is to note that the people directly involved may not have the most dispassionate appraisals of how these watershed events occurred. If they don't want to condemn themselves to a future of tedious barroom arguments with the grizzled, and somewhat cranky, holdouts from the 1989 fax glory days, or the true believers of the Radio Free Europe revolution, then today's cyber-utopians need to log off their Facebook accounts and try a little harder.

> "[Although] the long-term prospects of those in countries currently making the transition to democracy may be positive, this is of little comfort where the regime is willing to brutally crush dissent, as in Syria."

Corrupt Economic Policies Were the Driving Force Behind the Arab Spring

Matthew Partridge

Matthew Partridge is a journalist who contributes to the New Statesman *and other publications. In the following viewpoint, he contends that a key motivation for the Arab Spring has been the corrupt policies of the ruling class in many Arab countries. These corrupt economic policies, Partridge illustrates, exacerbated economic inequality, unemployment, and economic stagnation. Partridge argues that the political revolution and reform spreading through the Arab world must address economic justice and root out corruption or the political momentum will stall.*

As you read, consider the following questions:

1. How does Dr. Ali Kadri cite overall economic growth in the Arab world from 1971 to 2000?

2. What three Arab countries have some of the highest levels of economic inequality in the world, according to the viewpoint?

3. According to the International Labour Organization, how many of those of working age in the Middle East are employed?

Six months ago a Tunisian street seller started what is now known as the "Arab Spring" by setting himself on fire. However, although the immediate motivation behind his gesture was anger at the confiscation of his market stall, the economic causes of recent events in the Middle East have still received relatively little attention. However, many analysts believe that economic stagnation has been an important driving force behind the demands for political change, and that political and economic reform have to take place simultaneously.

An Expert's View

One expert who has extensively studied the interaction between development and politics in the Middle East is Dr Ali Kadri, the former head of the economic analysis section of the United Nations regional office in Beirut. Dr Kadri sees recent events in the Middle East as the culmination of decades of underdevelopment, and in some cases de-development, fuelled by failed economic policies and broken institutions. He points out that between 1971 to 2000 overall economic growth in the Arab world was negative, with the real GDP [gross domestic product] per capita [per person] of Gulf countries contracting by 2.8% annually.

At the same time inequality has increased, further squeezing the incomes of middle-class and working families. Although most Middle Eastern countries attempt to hide the extent of these problems by refusing to carry out the necessary surveys, unofficial reports suggest that the region is more unequal than even Africa or Latin America. According to the University of Texas Inequality Project, Qatar, Oman and Egypt had Gini coefficients [a way of measuring how something is dispersed, in statistical terms, developed by Italian sociologist Corrado Gini] of 55, 52 and 50 respectively in 2002, one of the highest levels in the world.

Corrupt Economic Policies

Kadri believes that these problems have been compounded through patronage. Lacking democratic legitimacy, "regimes in the region have used public sector employment to generate consent via clientelism . . . shifting the accent away from development". Although he believes that a degree of government ownership may be necessary in the short run, many of the state-run firms that dominate most Middle Eastern economies are focused on creating make-work jobs rather than productive goods.

These views are increasingly recognised by other organisations. In the case of Egypt, a US State Department document three years ago [2008] noted "the military's strong influence in Egypt's economy" and that "military-owned companies, often run by retired generals, are particularly active in the water, olive oil, cement, construction, hotel and gasoline industries". Similarly, a study by the World Bank of the Egyptian financial system found that because a significant portion of bank credit went to state companies, "family owned firms and small and medium enterprises rely heavily on the informal market".

Corruption and Employment Rates

These policies have resulted in high rates of unemployment and underemployment, especially among the young. According to the International Labour [Organization], less than half

The Point of the Arab Spring

The West wants to see democracy flourish in the Arab world, no doubt to protect its interests. But the locals want jobs, a better future for themselves and their families, a fairer distribution of the country's resources, and an end to corruption and police brutality. They want good governance and a respect for their traditions rather than Western-style democracy or Western interference.

Patrick Seale,
"The Rise of Political Islam," Middle East Online,
October 25, 2011. www.middle-east-online.com.

those of working age in the Middle East are actually in employment, with youth unemployment over four times the adult rate. Even in oil-rich Saudi Arabia, 30.2% of those between the ages of 20 and 24 are unemployed. Kadri believes that "those protesting want a dignified living and good schools for their children".

Kadri believes that corruption and regional conflict, which many analysts believe are consequences of dictatorships, have made it hard for firms to think beyond the short term. Kadri notes that the dearth of domestic investment opportunities has meant that much of the wealth generated by rising commodity prices over the last decade has gone abroad. He also suggests that the growing gap between savings and investment rates has been instrumental in producing financial bubbles, such as the speculative frenzy surrounding property and office construction in Dubai, which came to a dramatic end three years ago.

Kadri is relatively optimistic about the future of the region, suggesting that the collapse of autocrats, like [Zine El

Abidine] Ben Ali in Tunisia, will allow the population, rather than the elites, to determine the course of development for the first time. His conclusions are supported by World Bank research which found that the existence of an independent civil society was the most important factor in determining whether countries in central and eastern Europe were able to make a quick and successful economic transition after the fall of the Berlin Wall.

Making Political Change Work

However, although the long-term prospects of those in countries currently making the transition to democracy may be positive, this is of little comfort where the regime is willing to brutally crush dissent, as in Syria. Even in Egypt, there are signs that [President Hosni] Mubarak's machine is silently reconstituting itself, although its creator is now in jail. Although the G8 [a group of leaders from eight of the world's leading economies] has announced $40bn in economic support, much of this will come from Gulf countries who have little interest in economic and political change. This prompts the question of what else Western countries can do to make sure the political momentum generated by the "Arab Spring" continues and is able to result in rising living standards for all those in the region.

| *"These revolutions were not propagated by well-educated youth; these uprisings were spurred by the needs and demands of poorly educated youth, whose knowledge and skills do not meet the demands of a rapidly advancing world."* |

Education Played a Key Role in the Arab Spring

Anda Adams and Rebecca Winthrop

Anda Adams is an associate director at the Brookings Institution's Center for Universal Education, and Rebecca Winthrop is a director at the Center for Universal Education. In the following viewpoint, they suggest that the poor quality of education that most students receive in Arab countries is at the heart of the Arab uprisings. Adams and Winthrop acknowledge that many countries in the region have put more money in education and that students are attending school longer than in years before; however, the authors contend, their schooling is often of poor quality and irrelevant to the needs of today's marketplace. There is a clear need in the Arab world for an educational system that

focuses on the quality, relevancy, and equity of educational op-
portunities, which will go a long way in addressing the needs of
protesters across the region, the authors assert.

As you read, consider the following questions:

1. What percentage of the population of the Middle East
   and North Africa do the authors say is under the age of
   twenty?

2. What percentage of students in the Middle Eastern region transition to secondary education, according to the
   viewpoint?

3. According to the authors, what is the estimated number
   of youths in the Middle East by 2035?

The causes of the recent revolutions in the Arab world are
numerous and complex, and certainly cannot be attrib-
uted to one factor. Many experts spoke about the big role that
social media played; others addressed the deep-seated frustra-
tions with corruption, state legitimacy and foreign policies.

However, one tipping point that experts have focused on is
demographics—specifically, the youth bulge. Nearly one-half
of the population of the Middle East and North Africa is under the age of 20 and high rates of unemployment (25 percent)
among 15- to 24-year-olds in the region continues to be of
huge concern. While access to education is an essential path-
way out of poverty in many countries, in Morocco and Algeria, university graduates are less likely to be employed than
their peers who have only completed primary or secondary
school. In Egypt and Bahrain, those with a secondary school
education have higher rates of unemployment than their peers
with just primary school educations.

Education has played an important role in the uprisings in
the Middle East and North Africa with many commentators
noting that educated youth have been integral to what has

come to be called the "Arab Spring." However, what they fail to mention is that spending many years in school has failed to give many Arab youth a good education. These revolutions were not propagated by well-educated youth; these uprisings were spurred by the needs and demands of poorly educated youth, whose knowledge and skills do not meet the demands of a rapidly advancing world. Arab governments generally have allocated a significant portion of their national income to education; Djibouti, Tunisia, Morocco, Saudi Arabia, and Yemen each spend more than 5 percent of their gross national product on education. This has led to significant progress toward universal access to school; the regional gross enrollment ratio in primary school in 2008 was 96 percent (although the gender disparity is worth noting, with boys at 100 percent gross enrollment rate and girls at 91 percent). Ninety-seven percent survive to the last grade of primary school and then 95 percent of those transition to secondary education. Yet, there has been very low return on investment in terms of meaningful educational outcomes. Education systems throughout the region are hindered by low quality, irrelevancy and inequity.

Poor Quality Education and Lack of Proper Training

Low Quality. Internationally comparable reading test scores at grade 4 show that, in Kuwait, Qatar and Morocco, over 90 percent of the students scored lower than the minimum benchmark, which indicates that these students have not acquired basic reading comprehension after at least four years of schooling. The results do not improve over time either. Math and science scores for grade 8 show that the majority of students in Algeria, Egypt, Saudi Arabia, Syria and Qatar are below the minimum threshold. These students lack a basic understanding of whole numbers, decimals and simple graphs. According to Kevin Watkins [a senior fellow at the Brookings

Institution], education systems in the Middle East and North Africa are plagued by: teachers who are poorly trained, as well as poorly regarded in society; an emphasis on rote learning over critical thinking; and curriculum that seeks to train students to either work in the public sector—where the number of jobs are quickly diminishing—or continue on to postsecondary education, which most students are not able to do for a myriad of reasons.

Irrelevancy. This mismatch of skills learned in school and those needed in the workplace has led to the proliferation of "waithood," which refers to the increasingly common period of time that Arab youth have between graduation and getting their first job. Part of the unemployment problem is supply since these countries are not generating enough skilled jobs to absorb the increase in the educated labor force. But the other half of the problem is preparing young people with the necessary skills for jobs available. This is dependent upon the quality and relevancy of the education provided, particularly in the postprimary years. Research linking education to employment for Arab youth shows that one-third of them cannot do basic arithmetic and two-thirds of them self-reported that they didn't have the skills they needed to get a good job. Education systems are largely preparing students for employment in government bureaucracies where there is little job opportunity but not for the range of private sector work available.

Inequity. Although the attention in recent months has focused on the educated youth in the Arab world, there are still millions of children from poor households who are out of school. Their educational needs and rights cannot be ignored. This region also has some of the largest gender gaps with boys' enrollment and completion often far exceeding that of girls. In Egypt, girls from poor families living in the rural Upper Egypt region are doubly disadvantaged; half of them receive fewer than four years of schooling and one-quarter of them have fewer than two years of schooling.

Five Core Principles of "Quality of Education for All"

- That quality of education is the capacity of education systems to provide learners with the knowledge, skills, competencies and ethical and citizenship values which enable and qualify them to be active citizens.

- Improving quality of education always requires a long road of reforms, strong and consistent political leadership and sustained and predictable financing. . . .

- Improving education quality is the highest impact and most cost-effective national investment for any country in the Arab world, regardless of its level of economic development and income.

- The benefits resulting from successful educational reform far outweigh its costs, whatever its size, considering that the high economic output and returns of improving the performance of human resources reduces the impact of economic fluctuations and cyclical crises.

- The extra attention that needs to be provided to children living in emergency and special situations is also required in order to achieve quality of education for all.

"Doha Declaration: 'Quality of Education for All,'"
Arab Ministers of Education Meeting in Doha, Qatar,
September 21–22, 2010.

There is clear need for the Arab world and the broader global community to focus on the quality, relevancy, and equity of educational opportunities, particularly during adolescence. This is highlighted in the Center for Universal Education's new report "A Global Compact on Learning: Taking Action on Education in Developing Countries." Improving learning outcomes and education quality will require concerted focus and collective action. First, young children must get an early start on learning in life with quality early childhood development programs. Second, children must learn basic literacy and numeracy skills in the lower primary grades in order to continue and succeed in school. Third, young people must complete primary school and have access to educational opportunities that equip them with the necessary knowledge and skills to live safe, healthy, and productive lives.

Six Areas for Action

The emergence of a global learning crisis and waning international support for education lead us to call for a new global compact on learning that provides a broad framework and a series of targeted actions to improve learning opportunities and outcomes for all children and youth, especially the most marginalized. The global compact seeks to mobilize the international community—including developing and developed country governments, multilateral actors, private sector foundations and businesses, and local and international civil society—to put learning at the center of the global education agenda. Bold action and commitment are needed from all groups working together to embrace the following six principles:

- *Leadership* from developing and developed countries, as well as from heads of foundations, corporations and NGOs [nongovernmental organizations], must deliver and act on one clear consistent message: that learning matters for all children and youth, even the hardest to reach.

- *Partnership* among actors committed to improving learning in the developing world must leverage efforts to maximize the impact and ensure that everyone is pulling in the same direction.

- *Financing* is needed to achieve learning for all, which means that more resources must be dedicated while existing resources are used more effectively.

- *Measurement* of learning achievement in a way that can track progress against existing disparities and provide useful and timely insight for classroom-level practices is essential to fulfilling these goals.

- *Advocacy* that mobilizes public opinion to send strong signals to governments on the importance of learning for all and then holds those governments—developing and developed—accountable for the results.

- *Building* evidence to answer remaining questions about how to improve education and then using that information to scale up proven solutions for tackling the learning crisis.

Quality education and learning alone won't eliminate all the concerns of the youth protesters in the Middle East. But without greater attention to the real issues related to quality, relevancy, and equity in the education systems of these countries, the youth bulge that is estimated to reach 100 million by 2035 will be a challenge for the region, rather than an opportunity for a prosperous future.

Periodical and Internet Sources Bibliography

The following articles have been selected to supplement the diverse views presented in this chapter.

Elizabeth Dickinson	"Tunisia's Democracy Blooms as Model for Arab Spring," *Christian Science Monitor*, November 12, 2011.
Kevin Govern	"The Twitter Revolutions: Social Media in the Arab Spring," Jurist, October 22, 2011. http://jurist.org.
Josef Joffe	"The Arab Spring and the Palestine Distraction," *Wall Street Journal*, April 26, 2011.
Spencer Mandel	"Let Them Eat Baklava: Food Prices and the Arab Spring," Common Dreams, August 28, 2011. www.commondreams.org.
D. Parvaz	"The Arab Spring, Chronicled Tweet by Tweet," Al Jazeera, November 6, 2011. www.aljazeera .com.
Henry Porter	"The Arab Spring Will Only Flourish if the Young Are Given Cause to Hope," *Guardian* (UK), October 22, 2011.
Raymond Schillinger	"Social Media and the Arab Spring: What Have We Learned?," *Huffington Post*, September 20, 2011. www.huffingtonpost.com.
Kate Taylor	"Arab Spring Really Was Social Media Revolution," TG Daily, September 13, 2011. www.tgdaily.com.
Rami Zurayk	"Use Your Loaf: Why Food Prices Were Crucial in the Arab Spring," *Observer* (UK), July 16, 2011.

CHAPTER 2

How Should
the International
Community Respond
to the Arab Spring?

Chapter Preface

In 1945 Europe was devastated by years of brutal warfare during World War II. Relentless air attacks had flattened entire cities and industrial areas. Agricultural areas had been laid waste, and famine loomed over Western Europe. Economies in Germany, France, Belgium, Italy, and several other countries had been decimated. American government officials began to worry that the instability in Western Europe was dangerous and posed a real threat to US national security. They had seen the result of what had happened in Germany in the 1930s when the economy plummeted and people became fearful about their own safety—the rise of the Nazi Party and the emergence of Adolf Hitler. US president Harry Truman came to the realization that it was within America's self-interest to formulate a large-scale plan to provide economic assistance to Europe.

While the United States and the United Nations provided financial and humanitarian aid, the newly appointed secretary of state, George Marshall, was tasked with putting together a European aid package. Born in 1880 in Uniontown, Pennsylvania, Marshall graduated from the Virginia Military Institute and distinguished himself as a strategist and key planner of the American military efforts against Germany on the western front in World War I. He was appointed army chief of staff in 1939 and was instrumental in facilitating the development of the US Army into the most modern, best-equipped, and most efficient fighting force in the world. Marshall was lauded for his ability to coordinate Allied efforts in Europe and the Pacific. After the Allied victory in 1945, President Harry Truman sent Marshall to China to broker peace in the Chinese civil war—an effort that failed. On his return to the United States in 1947, Marshall was appointed secretary of state.

Marshall immediately put together a team to develop a plan to aid Europe. He recruited a number of experts in the field, including historian and diplomat George Kennan and William Clayton, a successful businessman and government official. Both men had prominent roles in shaping the final economic aid package, which was officially titled the European Recovery Program. On June 6, 1947, Marshall gave a speech at Harvard that introduced the European Recovery Program, which quickly became known as the Marshall Plan.

The Marshall Plan provided nearly $13 billion in aid to sixteen European countries, including Germany, which was spent to rebuild infrastructure and industrial areas; buy food, machinery, and fuel; and revive industrial production in Europe. By the time it ended in 1951, the Marshall Plan was widely hailed for rebuilding Europe's economic base and providing political, economic, and social stability in the region after World War II.

Today a number of world figures have been talking about creating a Marshall Plan for the Arab world, an area that has undergone tremendous political, economic, and social upheaval as a result of the Arab Spring. As countries in the region have struggled to root out endemic political corruption, enact social and economic justice, and implement democratic reform, many officials are concerned about the area's political and economic future. These officials argue that a large-scale economic package provided by developed countries in the West would go a long way to provide stability and establish long-lasting and enduring ties between the West and the Arab world.

The merit of a modern-day Marshall Plan is one of the topics included in the following chapter, which explores how the international community should respond to the Arab Spring. Other viewpoints in the chapter debate international intervention in Libya, strengthening anticorruption efforts, and applying universal human rights standards in the region.

> *"With corrupt rulers stealing billions per year from their people, the international community must develop methods to counter corruption while they remain in power."*

The International Community Must Strengthen Anticorruption Efforts in the Arab World

Stuart Levey

Stuart Levey is a senior fellow for national security and financial integrity at the Council on Foreign Relations. In the following viewpoint, he maintains that the international community can help fight the corruption that ravaged a number of Arab countries and led to the protests of the Arab Spring. Levey suggests that the international community should build on recent improvements to corruption laws in Switzerland, which passed the world's toughest law regarding returning money in Swiss banks to countries from which it was stolen by corrupt leaders. He rec-

Stuart Levey, "Fighting Corruption After the Arab Spring," *Foreign Affairs,* June 16, 2011. Reprinted by permission of FOREIGN AFFAIRS. Copyright 2011 by the Council on Foreign Relations, Inc. www.ForeignAffairs.com.

ommends that the United States and its allies should pressure other countries to adopt harsh regulations when it comes to stolen money and ill-gotten gains from corrupt leaders around the world.

As you read, consider the following questions:

1. How did Swiss banks become the top choice for corrupt dictators, according to Levey?

2. According to World Bank estimates, how much money do corrupt regimes steal from developing countries each year?

3. How many countries does the author say are now subjected to the assessments of the Financial Action Task Force (FATF)?

From Tunisia to Yemen, the corruption of Middle Eastern regimes has played a significant role in motivating the Arab Spring. Former Tunisian president Zine El Abidine Ben Ali and his family now face trial in absentia for, among other crimes, money laundering and drug trafficking. Meanwhile, Egyptian courts have charged former president Hosni Mubarak with corruption and sentenced in absentia his former finance minister, Youssef Boutros-Ghali, to 30 years in prison on charges of corruption and embezzlement of public money. Frustration with cronyism and corruption is a key grievance of those protesting in the streets in Libya, Syria, and Yemen as well.

These corrupt leaders have managed to stash much of their collected wealth abroad, despite international obligations designed to prevent such looting. The Arab Spring has thus highlighted the inadequacy of current international efforts against corruption.

Switzerland

If global leaders are serious about strengthening anticorruption efforts in response to the Arab Spring, they should build on recent improvements in an unlikely place: Switzerland. Switzerland recently changed its law about returning corrupt funds and has led much of the international community in freezing the assets of certain deposed leaders, including Ben Ali, Mubarak, and former Ivory Coast president Laurent Gbagbo. Switzerland took these actions at least in part because it feared that its reputation as a haven for illicit assets could harm its ability to attract legitimate business. The United States and its allies should capitalize on such reputational sensitivities by promoting mutually enforced anticorruption standards and exposing those countries that fail to cooperate. This is the most promising path to inducing countries to prevent corruption and to excluding the proceeds of corruption from the global financial system.

Swiss banks became known as a top choice for corrupt dictators by holding the multimillion-dollar accounts of, among others, former Nigerian ruler Sani Abacha, former Filipino president Ferdinand Marcos, and former Haitian strongman Jean-Claude Duvalier. Thus, it may come as a surprise that last October [2010], Switzerland adopted what is arguably the world's toughest law for repatriating the ill-gotten gains of corrupt politicians to the people of those countries, allowing the country to return potentially corrupt assets more easily.

The Arab Spring has thus highlighted the inadequacy of current international efforts against corruption.

The Challenges of Stopping the Corruption

Returning the fruits of corruption to their country of origin is a difficult undertaking. In the first place, the process of tracing and repatriation does not begin unless and until the corrupt regime is removed from power (obviously, a ruling regime depositing the money is highly unlikely to request such an investigation). Even when assets are located, legal obstacles often complicate repatriation. The new leadership in the country of origin may not be sufficiently independent of the old regime to pursue the matter, or may be unable to provide adequate proof that the assets in question were illicitly derived. As a result, only a relatively small amount of money has actually been returned to countries of origin. The World Bank estimates that corrupt regimes steal $20–$40 billion from developing countries each year; only $5 billion has been returned to those countries over the past 15 years.

The new Swiss law, known as the Restitution of Illicit Assets Act, took effect in February [2011] and addresses some of these problems by giving the Swiss government more freedom of action to repatriate questionable funds. For example, the new law shifts the burden of proof—the countries of origin are not required to prove the illicit nature of the funds. In situations where the wealth of a politician in question has increased dramatically during his reign and corruption is endemic in his country, the new law requires the politician to prove that he earned his wealth legitimately. Beyond improving the likelihood of restitution in specific cases, this law might persuade corrupt politicians to place their illicit assets elsewhere.

Switzerland's Reputation as a Global Financial Center

Switzerland hopes that its strengthened restitution law will do just that. The Swiss foreign ministry website states that "it is in Switzerland's fundamental interest to ensure that the assets of politically exposed persons obtained by unlawful means shall not be invested in the Swiss financial center." This, the ministry explains, is because "competition between financial centers is global. In the long term, it is a financial center's reputation and credibility that are the most important criteria with respect to competitors."

Like other nations, Switzerland undoubtedly realizes that a reputation for shielding corrupt assets can discourage legitimate investors, who may be deterred by the lack of transparency or by the prospect of being stigmatized by placing their money in a known destination for corrupt funds. Investors may also fear that a jurisdiction's poor reputation may attract greater regulatory and law enforcement scrutiny. A suspect reputation may also complicate the ability of a country's financial institutions to conduct business abroad, especially in the United States.

It is easy to be cynical about Switzerland's attempts to portray itself as a world leader in preventing corrupt politicians from hiding their money, given the country's history. But indulging that cynicism would risk missing the opportunity represented by Switzerland's desire to improve its reputation. With corrupt rulers stealing billions per year from their people, the international community must develop methods to counter corruption while they remain in power. Repatriation of funds only after a corrupt regime falls is insufficient. To ensure that effective preventive measures are taken, the international community should harness the dynamic that motivated Switzerland to reform—its desire to demonstrate the integrity of its financial system—to incentivize other nations to act.

The United Nations Convention Against Corruption

A multilateral commitment to improve anticorruption regulations exists. A hundred and forty nations have signed the United Nations Convention Against Corruption (UNCAC), a 2005 agreement that mandates a comprehensive vision for fighting corruption. Its signatories committed to adopting measures to prevent corruption such as creating anticorruption bodies, maintaining an independent judiciary, and establishing transparent procurement systems; criminalizing bribery and the embezzlement of public funds, and providing for the freezing and confiscation of the proceeds of those crimes; cooperating with other countries to enforce anticorruption laws and to return looted assets to their country of origin; and implementing rules to protect the financial system from the proceeds of corruption.

Unfortunately, there is no credible mechanism to ensure that countries implement the UNCAC. The implementation process sounds like a parody of an ineffective UN process: It relies on a "non-intrusive" "desk review" of a "comprehensive self-assessment checklist" completed by each signatory. A visit by an assessor to the country being reviewed can be made only if that country agrees. Reports on a country under investigation remain confidential unless the country under review chooses to have it published. On top of that, at the current pace, the first round of assessments will take 15 years to complete.

Other Anticorruption Efforts

Other well-intentioned anticorruption efforts similarly lack sufficient implementation mechanisms. Although a G-20 [group of twenty finance ministers and central bank governors from nineteen industrialized countries and the European Union] anticorruption "action plan" announced last November calls for countries to report back to G-20 leaders, it lacks a formal process to ensure concrete improvements. And the Organisation for Economic Co-operation and Development's existing assessment of whether its members are allowing companies to bribe foreign public officials does not extend to potential corruption issues within any member country itself.

Although the implementation of a comprehensive set of anticorruption measures undoubtedly poses daunting political challenges, there is an existing model that works: the global effort to combat money laundering and terrorist financing by the Financial Action Task Force (FATF). By publishing expert-created standards to combat illicit finances which are enforced by rigorous mutual evaluations among members, FATF has created a perpetual race to the top, or at least a race away from the bottom, as countries continuously seek to improve their FATF evaluations. The FATF consisted of only 16 members when first formed by the G-7 [group of finance ministers from seven industrialized countries] in 1989; today, more than 180 countries subject themselves to its or its affiliates' assessments. Its efforts are viewed as nonpolitical and are thus respected. Most important, FATF publishes its evaluation reports and its conclusions about which countries pose a risk to the system. Financial institutions around the globe pay close attention to FATF's assessments and use them to decide whether or how to operate in specific countries. Countries' fears of landing on one of FATF's warning lists, and their intense desire to remove themselves from those lists once named, are powerful motivators for self-improvement.

The international community could make real progress in combating corruption if an organization with FATF's credibility were empowered to set standards and assess countries' performance on the types of measures established in the UN-CAC. Such a process should build on the key lesson of Switzerland's reforms: The best way to motivate countries to prevent corruption is to harness their own desire to protect their reputations.

"The failure to implement reform results not only in the public's loss of confidence in the government, but also in a rivalry between political factions and threatened regimes to use religion as a source of legitimacy."

The International Community Should Foster Democratic Principles in the Arab World

Irena L. Sargsyan

Irena L. Sargsyan is a research analyst at the Saban Center for Middle East Policy at the Brookings Institution. In the following viewpoint, she recommends that the international community can help the countries involved in the Arab Spring move forward by providing resources and training to conduct fair and open elections, promote pluralistic governance, and facilitate the integration of political sects and parties. Sargsyan argues that such help is integral to cement the institutions of democracy in these countries and to counter the influence of repressive Islamist parties that will be looking to grab political and economic power.

As you read, consider the following questions:

1. Who does the author say is the leader of Sudan?

2. What was Black October in Algeria, according to the viewpoint?

3. According to the author, why has the Palestinian terrorist group Hamas declined in popularity?

The confluence of recent events in the Arab world—popular uprisings, political upheavals, and the emasculation of al-Qaeda—has put some in Washington in a bind, with policy makers applauding the democratic sweep but nervous that Islamist parties could gain power and subvert democratization. Indeed, the Middle East's and North Africa's own recent history offers important reasons to worry about the use of Islam in politics. But, as this history shows, the peril during times of political turmoil is not simply that Islam is used to advance extremist agendas, but that it is used to mask deficiencies in governance, legitimacy, and accountability.

The major concern for some in the United States is that Islamist parties—the strongest opposition party in Egypt and a growing force in Tunisia—are positioned to gain political power in the upcoming elections.

But Islamicization of politics is most likely to occur when a new government fails to carry out its promises of political, economic, and social reforms—not when Islamist opposition parties run in elections. The failure to implement reform results not only in the public's loss of confidence in the government, but also in a rivalry between political factions and threatened regimes to use religion as a source of legitimacy. Repression is often the next step.

Religion Is a Means to an End

In Sudan, for example, after the government failed to carry out reforms and instead enforced Islamic law throughout the country during the early 1980s, civil war resumed between

Muslims in the north and non-Muslims in the south. Army generals, who sought to strengthen their domestic positions in the wake of Arab defeats in regional wars, pressured political leaders to continue implementing harsh Islamic practices. Gen. Omar al-Bashir, a devout Islamist who overthrew the democratically elected prime minister Sadiq al-Mahdi in a 1989 coup, has presided over the continuing Islamicization of Sudan.

Even staunchly secular regimes often turn to Islam to bolster their legitimacy when repression proves insufficient to resolve a legitimacy crisis. Saddam Hussein's attempts to suppress Iraq's Shiite population—most brutally in 1991 and again in 1999—de-legitimized the Iraqi leader and his Ba'ath Party. To gain Shiite support, Saddam launched the so-called "Faith" campaign in the 1990s. He added quotes from the Quran to his public speeches, constructed lavish mosques, banned the consumption of alcohol, and ordered the inclusion of religious symbols in the mass media.

Iraq and Algeria

In post-Saddam Iraq, Prime Minister Nouri al-Maliki has had to contend with the largest Islamist movement—headed by opposition leader Muqtada al-Sadr—which delivers water, electricity, and protection in impoverished areas of Iraq. As al-Maliki competes with al-Sadr over the Sadrist popular base, he repeatedly claims that he and his Dawa Party—founded by another member of the al-Sadr family—are the legitimate voice of Islam.

As these examples show, leaders often use Islam as a political tool to avoid reform, or when reform proves too difficult to implement. The same risk holds true for countries transitioning to democratic systems of government. A case in point is Algeria.

When Algeria won its independence from France in 1962, after eight years of fighting, the socialist-oriented Front de

Libération Nationale (FLN) came to power. But its internecine rivalries and inability to manage Algeria's myriad problems—including high unemployment, rampant corruption, demographic pressures, and rising foreign debt—triggered popular uprisings. In 1988 the revolts culminated in an event known as Black October—an uprising of Algerian youth that was brutally suppressed by the country's armed forces. After hundreds of protesters died and many Islamic activists were arrested (some were tortured), the FLN and Algeria's politicized military lost the legitimacy that they had earned in the war for independence.

"Islam is the solution" became the slogan in the country, and religious rather than revolutionary credentials became the source of legitimacy. And after the Front Islamique du Salut achieved significant electoral gains in 1990 and 1991, the military obstructed elections, banned Islamist parties, installed a new president, and purged the FLN of all leaders in favor of democracy. Many prominent FLN leaders, who had once criticized the idea that Islam should play a part in government, abandoned socialism and invoked Islamist ideology to boost their religious credibility.

What the United States Can Do

To preclude events that can derail democratization today, the United States should help the states now in transition to foster democratic principles, liberal institutions, vigorous civil societies, and respect for human rights and civil liberties. The international community should provide resources and training to promote healthy pluralistic governance, competitive elections, and political integration. Nascent political parties should be encouraged to become as well organized as some of their Islamist counterparts.

Islamist parties, in turn, should be included in the political process, so that they can share responsibility for their country's successes and failures in governance, defense, and foreign af-

© 2011 Arend Van Dam and PoliticalCartoons.com.

fairs. Though some thinkers in U.S. foreign policy circles urge the sequestering of Islamists—such as the Muslim Brotherhood in Egypt—this approach will ultimately backfire. When Islamist groups are marginalized as the opposition, they become a viable channel for expressing political dissent and popular grievances. Case in point: Hamas. As long as Palestinian Hamas was an opposition movement, its political appeal continued to grow, enabling its electoral victory in 2006. But Hamas's failure to govern effectively has led to a steady decline in its popularity.

Equally important, the United States should not conflate moderate mainstream Islamist political parties with Islamist fundamentalists. To equate the two is not only imperceptive, but consequential as well. The moderates support socioeconomic reform and the prevention of terrorism; many also endorse democratic governance. The fundamentalists are a minority, significantly less popular in countries with strong national and Arab identities. Distinguishing between moderates and fundamentalists would prevent new regimes in the

Middle East and North Africa from resorting to repressive survival strategies in the name of fighting an Islamist threat—which is how many of their predecessors stayed in power.

Take the Opportunity

Recent developments in the Middle East and North Africa have produced an unprecedented opening for change that will not last. The international community has both the opportunity and the responsibility to facilitate transformation in the countries that seek democratization. This historic moment—the Arab Spring—is no time for inaction.

If history is any guide, the use of Islam in the political arena might not be a sign that countries such as Egypt or Tunisia are adopting more extremist agendas, but that their governments are incapable of fulfilling the promises they made to their people.

The [President Barack] Obama administration, the U.S. Congress, and indeed, the international community should remain focused on each country in transition, recalibrate old policies toward the region, and take concrete, meaningful actions to support democratization now.

A failure to do so would disillusion millions of hopeful souls in the Middle East and North Africa—as well as create more instability in the world.

> *"The events of the Arab Spring empha-*
> *sise that people everywhere yearn to be*
> *free, to have their voices heard and to*
> *participate in the decisions that affect*
> *their lives."*

The International Community Should Apply Universal Human Rights Standards to the Arab Spring

Mary Robinson

Mary Robinson is the former president of Ireland and member of the Elders, a group of independent global leaders working together for peace and human rights. In the following viewpoint, she contends that the international community should not turn a blind eye to human rights violations and injustices in the Arab world in the belief that the region does not value ideals like freedom, justice, and human rights. In fact, Robinson argues, the Arab Spring shows that people in these countries are demanding governments that value such ideals. The international community, Robinson concludes, can help by holding Arab countries to the same human rights standards as Western countries.

As you read, consider the following questions:

1. When did former Tunisian president Zine El Abidine Ben Ali leave office, according to the viewpoint?

2. According to the author, how many Egyptians are still missing since the beginning of the Arab Spring?

3. What Burmese human rights leader expressed her hope that the Arab Spring would come to her oppressed country, according to the viewpoint?

It has been fascinating to return to Lebanon in the past few days, with its relatively free press and vibrant civil society. Yet, at the same time, I noticed little change in its political system—one that enables all factions to be represented, often by the descendants of the same families, which has a stultifying effect. What impact will the huge changes and volatility of the region have on this country and its people?

Looking out over a thousand young faces of the graduating class at the American University of Beirut, I was filled with hope. They understand profoundly the events around them and welcome the changes in their region. Their seriousness of purpose was palpable, but so was their enthusiasm for the challenges ahead in this new climate of freedom and human dignity.

It was moving to see so tangibly that they too are inspired by the sacrifices made by their brothers and sisters across the Arab world, who are risking their lives daily to demand justice and respect for fundamental human rights.

The events of the Arab Spring emphasise that people everywhere yearn to be free, to have their voices heard and to participate in the decisions that affect their lives. In particular, they show that these are not 'Western' values, but universal values to which we all aspire.

No More Double Standards

For too long, many authoritarian regimes have falsely claimed that certain values—freedom, justice, human rights—are 'Western'. And in pursuit of national and regional 'stability', many Western governments, while paying lip service to democratic ideals and human rights, have turned a blind eye to violations committed by leaders and governments with whom they enjoyed good relations. It is clear that this exceptionalism is fundamentally flawed. Citizens are adamant: They will no longer tolerate 'business as usual'.

This January [2011], following six weeks of popular protest, we witnessed what many Tunisians thought they would never see: the departure of President [Zine El Abidine] Ben Ali. One month later, Egypt's President Hosni Mubarak stepped down after Egyptians from all walks of life—men and women, rich and poor—took to the streets to demand an end to dictatorship and repression.

These protests spread across the Middle East and North Africa, but have not yet delivered the changes that people want. In Libya, Bahrain, Syria and Yemen, the violent response by states to legitimate demands from their citizens have cost many thousands of lives.

Courage and a Refusal to Be Silenced

The refusal of demonstrators to be silenced, in spite of the violent reactions they face, reflects the emergence of an active and increasingly confident citizenry in many Arab countries.

In Egypt, the revolution did not end with the downfall of Hosni Mubarak. Young people, unions, journalists and other civil society groups are still struggling to hold the country's interim military rulers to account. In just one example, uproar ensued when a blogger who was critical of military actions was jailed by a military tribunal. Protesters are now pushing for the release of all political prisoners and to know what has

Reflections on the Arab Spring from the United Nations High Commissioner for Human Rights

On 1 January this year [2011], the protests in Tunisia were multiplying, fuelled by the heavy-handed response of the Tunisian government, but President [Zine El Abidine] Ben Ali was still in power, and we had little inkling of the extraordinary chain of events that was about to be unleashed across North Africa and the Middle East, and which have reverberated all across the world.

A mere six weeks later, the peoples of Tunisia and Egypt had both risen up in defence of their rights and to everyone's surprise, not least their own, had succeeded in unseating their long-entrenched and deeply unpopular presidents, along with many other members of the corrupt and repressive ruling elite. Huge numbers of people in both countries had gone out onto the streets to call for their economic and social rights, as well as their rights to express themselves and to protest, and their rights not to be arbitrarily detained, tortured or killed. And they had prevailed.

The significance of this has been immense. The Middle East and North Africa was one of those areas where we had all been told the people had other preoccupations and were not particularly interested in human rights. Those of us who work in human rights had never believed that particular discourse, but it had nevertheless become deeply rooted, not just within the region but in the mind-set of the outside world as well.

Statement of Navi Pillay,
United Nations Office of the High Commissioner
for Human Rights, June 30, 2011.

happened to over 5,000 Egyptians missing—believed detained without trial by security services—since the unrest began.

The international community can and should help these burgeoning civil society movements. While an interventionist approach may be counterproductive, other countries can help protect the legitimacy of these movements by holding all governments to the universal standards that their citizens expect.

Global Solidarity

The popular uprisings in the Arab world have captivated and inspired others to a remarkable degree. Our sister Elder, Aung San Suu Kyi, spoke of the effect of the Arab Spring on the pro-democracy movement in Burma (http://www.bbc.co.uk/programmes/p00htkm3): "Do we envy the people of Egypt and Tunisia? Yes. . . . But more than envy is a sense of solidarity and of renewed commitment to our cause, which is the cause of all women and men who value human dignity and freedom."

In Egypt, the death of a young businessman at the hands of state security forces inspired thousands of Egyptians to protest in his name, saying, "We are all Khaled Said." This spirit of solidarity is multiplied as people around the world watch events in real time and amplify protesters' calls for freedom, democracy and human rights—thanks in no small part to the Internet and social media.

These tools not only help people organise civil society movements and share their experiences; they reaffirm the fact that when we demand our basic rights, we are not alone. We are justified in holding our governments to account, and in seeking to build inclusive and free societies that benefit the many, not the privileged few.

Whatever may transpire in the coming months and years across the Middle East and North Africa, the Arab Spring has shown us that universal values are not an abstract concept—they make a real, practical difference to people's lives. Most importantly, the protesters have shown us that these values are truly universal. They belong to each of us to fight for and to treasure.

> "*Economic grievances—including massive unemployment, unreasonable levels of inequality, and a huge youth bulge in many Arab countries—are galvanizing the Arab street to attempt to redraw the political landscape.*"

The International Community Should Launch an Arab Marshall Plan

Richard Javad Heydarian

Richard Javad Heydarian is a political analyst. In the following viewpoint, he argues that gross economic management and inequality is at the heart of the Arab Spring. He recommends that the international community steps in to offer a package of financial aid, based on the Marshall Plan that helped to rebuild Europe after World War II. Heydarian points out that this is in the best interest of the United States and its allies because it will facilitate the transition of the Arab region to democracy and protect them from the intervention of extremist reactionary ele-

ments. He views the Arab Spring as an opportunity for the West to encourage a more democratic region that will be friendly to Western interests.

As you read, consider the following questions:

1. According to the 2009–2010 economic competitiveness index, where did Tunisia rank on the scale of major economic liberalization and openness indexes?

2. What region does the author cite as having the highest level of unemployment in the world?

3. What does the author state are the two major economic reasons that oil-rich states in the Persian Gulf have so far been more adept at managing protests and calls for democratic reform?

There's no doubt the ongoing Middle Eastern revolutions make ample use of democratic slogans, encouraged by the civic spirit of millions that have marched for liberty and equality. Though many factors are contributing to the historic changes that are sweeping across the region, a combination of decades of aggressive economic liberalization and political repression has played a crucial role in mobilizing the masses against the hand of autocracy.

The overthrow of Arab despots is more a function of gross economic mismanagement and brutal political centralization than an inevitable result of some Hegelian [expressing reality in rational categories] unfolding of the motions of history. Economic grievances—including massive unemployment, unreasonable levels of inequality, and a huge youth bulge in many Arab countries—are galvanizing the Arab street to attempt to redraw the political landscape.

But Iran's standoff with the West and fears of another oil shock are tempering Western support for democratic protests in certain strategic countries, complicating U.S. foreign policy in the region.

Revolutions and Economic Crises

Revolutions rarely happen in stagnant, destitute countries. Recent history shows that revolutions are most likely to occur in countries that either experience a long period of unprecedented economic growth not accompanied by political reform or that undergo a sudden economic crisis following a sustained period of economic expansion. In the context of rising expectations and relative deprivation, the masses—mobilized by opposition forces—gradually withdraw their support of the regime, step outside their comfort zones, and increasingly embrace the opportunities and challenges of revolutionary upheavals.

After the 1997 East Asian financial crisis, food riots and antigovernment protests hit a number of autocratic regimes in the region. In Indonesia the economic crisis severely compromised the legitimacy of the [President] Suharto regime. Many were fed up with the repressive regime, and the autocracy's inability to provide economic security led to widespread riots, democratic protests, and the eventual collapse of the 30-year-old "New Order." In the Middle East, the 1979 Iranian revolution followed a similar track. After two decades of impressive economic growth, [the then leader of Iran] Mohammad Reza Shah's unwillingness to introduce meaningful political reforms—including changing the country's government to a constitutional monarchy by establishing an independent legislature—caught up with him. Coupled with growing economic inequality, an urban-rural schism, and unprecedented inflationary pressures—as a result of massive injections of petrodollar revenues into the domestic economy—pushed a restive population to the brink.

Parallels to the Arab Spring

The Arab Spring is arguably running along a similar pattern. The debt crisis in the 1980s served as an opportunity for international financial institutions (IFIs) to impose sweeping economic restructuring—in the form of structural adjustment programs (SAPs)—to many state-dominated economies in the Global South, including throughout the Middle East. The destructive eight-year Iran-Iraq war, a reduction in oil revenues, bloated bureaucracies, high levels of debt, and balance-of-payment crises pushed many countries in the region to undergo IFI-prescribed economic liberalization. The result was massive reductions in state subsidies, unprecedented levels of privatization, readjustments in trade patterns, and the transformation of the state from a paternalistic, welfare-oriented model into a regulatory-minimalist entity.

But unlike countries in Latin America, East Asia, and sub-Saharan Africa, the Middle East did not experience political reform after decades of economic liberalization. Instead, Arab autocrats used economic liberalization as an opportunity to transfer welfare responsibilities to the private sector, establish new patterns of patronage by favoring selected clients during bidding processes and privatization schemes, and enrich their military allies by granting them access to major businesses and investments. The product was crony capitalism: high levels of corruption, poor state services, and absence of a decisive and developmental state.

A False Economic Doctrine

In the last three decades, [Zine El Abidine] Ben Ali in Tunisia and Anwar Sadat and Hosni Mubarak in Egypt abandoned the more egalitarian and welfare-oriented policies of their predecessors in favor of economic opening and deregulation. The IMF [International Monetary Fund] and World Bank have touted Egypt and Tunisia's economic reform as regional cases of globalization's success. Both countries registered good scores on major economic liberalization and openness indexes. Both received good rankings in the 2009–10 economic competitiveness index.

Tunisia, ranked 32nd, placed above Lithuania, Brazil, and Turkey, while Egypt, ranked 70th, is higher than Greece and Croatia. In the KOF Globalization Index, which rates the diffusion of government policies, Egypt and Tunisia rank 12th and 35th respectively. Egypt, considered one of the hottest emerging economies in the world, is part of the CIVETS (Colombia, Indonesia, Vietnam, Egypt, Turkey, South Africa), and Tunisia has been a leading Arab country in free trade and economic liberalization. The two countries have been the face of economic globalization in the Arab world.

But in reality, economic liberalization allowed Tunisian and Egyptian autocrats to institute a mafia-like system that allowed favored cliques to dominate the tourism, real estate, and banking sectors. In both Tunisia and Egypt, the minimalist-regulatory doctrine imposed by IFIs prevented the state from becoming a central player in implementing industrial trade policies to foster sustained industrialization and economic growth. As a result, despite decades of impressive economic growth, a significant portion of the population is impoverished, and unemployment is sky-high. The absence of globally competitive industries meant that these countries were hugely dependent on sectors fraught with speculative practices, fraud, and uncertainty: real estate, banking, and tourism. Economic liberalization and regulatory capture (in which industries essentially control the state apparatus designed to regulate them) meant that the state had less budgetary and fiscal leverage to deal with sudden price rises in basic commodities. Due to rampant deregulation and openness, commodity prices in Tunisia and Egypt are increasingly determined by variables beyond national boundaries.

A Region in Crisis

The Arab world has the highest level of unemployment in the world, and youth unemployment rates are astronomical—averaging over 23 percent in the region. Worse, 60 percent of the Arab world is under the age of 30. In Tunisia, Egypt, Yemen, and potentially Jordan and Syria, the iron fists of repressive regimes were only able to postpone an inevitable political earthquake.

The recent global financial, food, and energy crises accentuated the failure of economic liberalization to adequately spread the region's wealth. Significant declines in the tourism, financial, and real estate sectors due to the financial crisis crippled the few well-functioning economic engines. Because the region's governments have little fiscal power—thanks to privatization, FDI [foreign direct investment]-friendly tax incentives, regulatory capture, and bureaucratic streamlining—and increasingly shied away from providing economic subsidies to benefit the populace, the food crisis over the last decade has pushed millions of people in food-importing Arab nations into abject poverty and hunger. Worsening matters, foreign aid from the developed world diminished as a result of the economic crisis.

The absence of democratic institutions in the Arab world prevented people from constructively airing their basic economic grievances. Faced with growing state brutality and deepening economic insecurity, more and more people joined the ranks of the antigovernment protesters who eventually toppled Ben Ali and Mubarak. In Tunisia and Egypt, labor unions bridged the gap between the Facebook-friendly middle class and the broader disenfranchised masses. Economic desperation served as the rallying cry around which all sectors and classes coalesced. Similar grievances are continuing to fuel protests across the Arab world.

Petropolitics and Democratization in the Persian Gulf

Unlike their resource-poor counterparts, oil-rich states in the Persian Gulf have so far been more adept at managing protests and calls for democratic reform. There are two major

The Marshall Plan After World War II

In the period between 1949 to 1951, a substantial amount of financial aid was poured into the European economy as a direct result of the Marshall Plan which had been drafted in the United States. These finances reached a tune of thirteen billion dollars at that time. The latter sum was labelled as the European Recovery Program. The Marshall Plan had been drafted and then approved by the United States Congress during the year 1948 under an act known as the Economic Cooperation Act. It took the US a period of three months to implement this program after it had been approved. Thereafter, the European Recovery Program took a period of three years to be executed in the European continent.

Carolyn Smith, "Importance of the Marshall Plan
to Economic Recovery in Europe in the Post War Era,"
Articlebase, March 1, 2010. www.articlesbase.com.

economic reasons for this: They enjoy substantial fiscal clout because of favorable oil prices in the last decade, and their strategic value—as major energy suppliers—to the West has muted the latter's response to crackdowns on peaceful protests, most notably in Bahrain.

Flush with billions of petrodollars, many Gulf Cooperation Council (GCC) [also known as the Cooperation Council for the Arab States of the Gulf] countries have doled out huge sums in order to stave off growing protests and appease basic economic grievances. In addition, the GCC has also helped its poorer members, Oman and Bahrain, use similar tactics by offering each of them $10 billion development package loans. With Libyan energy exports in tatters, and decreasing spare capacity in Saudi Arabia, many policy makers fear the possibility of another oil shock and a double-dip recession if the Arab Spring seriously affects supply in other major oil exporters. Poor countries dependent on remittances from migrant workers in the Middle East—like Nepal and the Philippines—could also suffer if revolutions upend the Persian Gulf status quo. Furthermore, Western views of Gulf protests are influenced by their desire for energy supplies—the stakes may simply be too high for Western countries to countenance upheaval in the Gulf.

Geopolitical factors—most notably Israeli security and the fear of unfriendly, radical groups gaining power—prevented the United States from immediately supporting calls for regime change in Egypt. In the Gulf, containment of Iran is the complicating geopolitical variable. Because many Gulf protesters are Shiite Muslims, the "Iran card" has been aggressively used by Arab monarchies to justify their brutal crackdowns. With the Saudi-led GCC intervention in Bahrain clearly targeted to stamp out any potential Iranian foothold, the Gulf Arab Spring is entering a dangerous stage. With key U.S. naval assets concentrated in the Gulf, Washington has been more reticent in condemning brutal attacks on protesters. U.S. ambiguity—despite some strongly worded criticisms of current crackdowns—has emboldened the GCC to viciously suppress genuine democratic demands by mainly Shia protesters in Bahrain. U.S. pressure was crucial in advancing democratic revolutions in Egypt and Tunisia, but Washington has been far from helpful for Gulf protesters. This has reinforced many protesters' views of the United States as a staunch supporter of oppressive regimes rather than a democracy promoter. Thus, a combination of economic and geopolitical factors is preventing democratic reform in the Persian Gulf. Thanks to America's regrettable passivity, democratic protests could increasingly turn anti-American.

A Marshall Plan for the Middle East

If economic issues mobilized the masses against autocracies, they could also compromise the potential for smooth democratic transitions. Tunisia and Egypt are still suffering from the impact of the global economic downturn as well as the instability brought about by their respective revolution, leading to the possibility of a counterrevolution by reactionary forces. In Egypt, remnants of the National Democratic Party and the organizationally potent Muslim Brotherhood could easily outmaneuver their more liberal counterparts if the situation remains unstable. European countries across the Mediterranean are wary of a mass exodus of Arabs fleeing political repression. Furthermore, the United States has no desire to see extremist political actors gain influence in the region.

Ideally, richer Arab countries would be the primary source of assistance for poorer countries undergoing democratic transitions. Qatar's creative foreign policy posture and influential Al Jazeera news network, for instance, have been very proactive in supporting opposition forces in Libya and across the Arab world. But Al Jazeera has been notably silent on the turmoil in Bahrain. And the other rich Arab countries, autocracies with nondemocratic agendas, are not likely to provide funds for new democratic movements.

The United States was pivotal in the reconstruction and democratic consolidation of Western Europe in the aftermath of World War II. In the 1970s, Western Europe played a crucial role in the democratic transition of its southern neighbors—Greece, Portugal, and Spain. The same success story was repeated in much of Eastern Europe after the Berlin Wall fell in 1989. Similar constructive efforts by the international community are needed for the Arab uprisings of 2011 to succeed. The current upheaval in the Middle East represents an intersection of geopolitical interests, energy security, and democratic values for the West. Thus, there is plenty of reason for Washington and its allies to contemplate launching an

Arab Marshall Plan. This might be the last and best opportunity for the West to facilitate the creation of another "island of peace"—a sympathetic democratic community in the much-troubled Arab world.

"The potential benefit of successfully backing the rebels will be an increase in goodwill across the Arab world directed at the West."

The International Community Should Have Intervened in Libya

Ahmed Moor

Ahmed Moor is a journalist. In the following viewpoint, written before the overthrow of the Muammar Gaddafi government in the fall of 2011, he suggests that international intervention in Libya is a legitimate decision for two reasons: the Libyan rebels requested aid from the outside world, and many people agree that the situation in Libya is horrifying and unsustainable. Moor emphasizes that a successful intervention would mean that the international community would take a backseat to the Libyan rebels, providing them with the support they need to overthrow the regime. Moor asserts that it also would mean refraining from trying to install a puppet government that would do the bidding of the West.

As you read, consider the following questions:

1. According to the author, who is to blame more than any other figure in the post-war twentieth century for eroding the gains in legitimacy for supranational institutions and their proponents?

2. In what year does the author say that the United States was able to strong-arm weaker states to invade Iraq?

3. What does the author see as the consequences of a successful revolution in Bahrain?

There is a lot about the Western intervention in Libya that could go wrong—and it remains to be seen whether bombing [Muammar] Gaddafi[1] and his mercenaries is a good decision.

However, large numbers of people around the world appear to support the objectives of the anti-regime forces. Also, the indigenous resistance movement—which requested help—would have been annihilated in the absence of those air strikes.

George [W.] Bush's legacy of destruction extends beyond the piles of brick, flesh and mortar that we have been tallying for a decade now in Iraq and Afghanistan.

More than any other figure in the post-war 20th century, the last American president did more to erode the gains in legitimacy made by supranational institutions and their proponents.

After the Iraq war, the United Nations [UN] began to be perceived as a US rubber-stamp body—or worse—as a meaningless exercise in bureaucracy.

The UN can only function legitimately through consensus (or consensus-like) decision making and it was clear that the US was strong-arming weaker states in 2003.

1. Libyan dictator Muammar Gaddafi was captured and killed by rebel forces near his hometown of Sirte on October 20, 2011.

George Bush and the neoconservatives hijacked the legitimate language of consensus-based intervention for their own ill use.

So activists are not wrong to react cynically when they hear that language today; I don't believe that bombing Gaddafi is a humanitarian gesture.

But George Bush should not be allowed to delegitimize the mechanisms—which are distinct from the language—of global intervention in situations that offend human rights and dignity.

Today, many people agree that the situation in Libya is horrifying. Furthermore, the Libyan rebels requested aid from the outside world.

Those two conditions alone do not justify intervention but they are crucial components of a legitimate international decision to employ force.

What Is a Successful Intervention?

The question of what a successful intervention means is a very important one. At the very least, it means taking a backseat and supporting the rebels in the capacity that they desire.

It also means not attempting to install a new government that's pliant and subordinate to the West. Compromise on these two principles will quickly diminish the legitimacy of the campaign against Gaddafi.

Many people have argued that the intervention is a Western imperialist project. Here, it is worth remembering that Western powers were already in control of Libya's oil when the revolution began.

Muammar Gaddafi was as much "our guy" as [Egyptian president] Hosni Mubarak. [Former secretary of state] Condoleezza Rice personally visited Libya and met with Gaddafi in 2008.

The following year [former British prime minister] Tony Blair pushed for the release of the Lockerbie bomber [referring to Libyan citizen Abdelbaset Ali Mohmed al-Megrahi who was convicted of killing 270 people when he placed a bomb on an airplane that exploded over Scotland] to secure a sweetheart deal with the Libyan regime (although it was [British prime minister] Gordon Brown who did the releasing).

Western powers would have been much better served by backing Gaddafi if oil was their object.

An Imperialist Argument

There is an alternative imperialism argument: that the intervention is really a push to consolidate Western control over Libyan resources. But, without intervention the rebels would have most certainly been annihilated by Gaddafi's superior forces.

So why back the losing horse? How can Western powers be sure they can succeed in creating a more agreeable government? Would not they go with the devil they know, especially when he is already their devil?

Finally, any government that takes shape in Libya in the future will have to address the basic issues that fueled the popular uprising there in the first place.

Gaddafi is an imperial stooge and a new imperial government will ensure that the underlying conditions will not go away.

Spreading Goodwill and Avoiding Oil Price Spikes

So what's motivating the Western powers into projecting their power into Libya? And why is the West not intervening in Bahrain or Saudi Arabia or Yemen?

The potential benefit of successfully backing the rebels will be an increase in goodwill across the Arab world directed at the West. It is not clear if that is a realistic expectation, but it is one that appears to motivate Western leaders.

Muammar Qaddhafi, the Former Ruler of Libya

Muammar Qaddhafi, the longtime leader of the oil-rich country of Libya, was one of the United States' major foes. Considered a zealot and terrorist, he was driven by the idea of a united Islamic "Arab nation" linking the region from the Persian Gulf to the north coast of Africa on the Atlantic Ocean. Qaddhafi, however, completed Libya's international rehabilitation in 2006 when the United States announced it would restore full diplomatic relations. Secretary of State Condoleezza Rice said the U.S. would drop its designation of Libya as a state sponsor of terrorism. Rice, according to the *New York Times*, cited "tangible results that flow from the historic decisions taken by Libya's leadership in 2003 to renounce terrorism and to abandon its weapons of mass destruction programs." However, Qaddhafi continued to rule Libya as a tyrant, and reports of criminal activity and the murder of Libyan citizens were brought forth to the International Criminal Court. An uprising in early 2011 forced Qaddhafi out of power by August of that year. On October 20, 2011, during a battle between his soldiers and the revolutionary fighters who had come to arrest him, the dictator was killed.

"Muammar Qaddhafi,"
Gale Biography in Context,
October 26, 2011.

Meanwhile, the cost of attacking Gaddafi and his mercenaries in a limited way and supplying the rebels with arms is relatively low. It is not clear if the cost is actually low, but it's likely that it is perceived that way since the intervention is already under way.

In Bahrain and Saudi Arabia, the opposite is true. The American president Barack Obama will seek reelection, so it is in his interest to prevent the global economy from stagnating then shrinking.

A successful revolution in Bahrain may destabilize Saudi Arabia which would drive the price of oil up which could cause the US economy to stall. It is just not a risk worth taking for him.

Probably, fears of an insurgent Iran—legitimate or not—play into his calculations as well. That's because most Bahrainis are Shias.

Yemen

Likewise, Yemen permits the Americans to pursue al Qaeda affiliates in that country. That goes directly to Obama's security credentials.

If Yemen lapses, Obama will be accused, rightly or wrongly, of permitting terrorist sympathizers to take control in yet another Middle Eastern country. And the 2012 election campaign is already under way.

Intervention in Libya could turn out badly in many different and unforeseen ways. And imperialism and neoliberal "reforms"—which are a problem in that country—did not arrive with the revolution; they preceded it.

We can aspire towards helping young Libyans reform their society to make it more democratic, just and anti-imperialist. But before they can do that they must survive Gaddafi's pulverizing onslaught. And that's something that the Western offensive gives them a chance of doing.

"*The point isn't just that Western intervention in Libya is grossly hypocritical. It's that such double standards are an integral part of a mechanism of global power and domination that stifles hopes of any credible international system of human rights protection.*"

The International Community Should Not Have Intervened in Libya

Seumas Milne

Seumas Milne is an associate editor and columnist for the Guardian. In the following viewpoint, written before the overthrow of the Muammar Gaddafi government and the subsequent killing of Gaddafi by rebel forces in the fall of 2011, Milne asserts that international intervention in the Libyan conflict was hypocritical, ineffective, and immoral. Milne suggests that Western justifications for the intervention based on humanitarian reasons are false; in fact, he maintains, it was motivated by the desire to get on the "right side of history" and to secure oil interests. He concludes that the intervention was a threat to the entire North African region.

As you read, consider the following questions:

1. According to the author, what percentage of British citizens polled were against the Libyan intervention as of March 2011?

2. How many people does the author estimate live in Benghazi?

3. What happened in Kosovo in 1999 after international intervention, according to the author?

It's as if it's a habit they can't kick. Once again US, British and other NATO [North Atlantic Treaty Organization] forces are bombarding an Arab country with cruise missiles and bunker-busting bombs. Both David Cameron [the prime minister of the United Kingdom] and [US president] Barack Obama insist this is nothing like Iraq. There will be no occupation. The attack is solely to protect civilians.

But eight years after they launched their shock-and-awe devastation of Baghdad and less than a decade since they invaded Afghanistan, the same Western forces are in action against yet another Muslim state, incinerating soldiers and tanks on the ground and killing civilians in the process.

Supported by a string of other NATO states, almost all of which have taken part in the Iraq and Afghanistan occupations, the US, Britain and France are clinging to an Arab fig leaf, in the shape of a Qatari air force that has yet to arrive, to give some regional credibility to their intervention in Libya.

Humanitarian Justifications

As in Iraq and Afghanistan, they insist humanitarian motives are crucial. And as in both previous interventions, the media are baying for the blood of a pantomime villain leader, while regime change is quickly starting to displace the stated mission. Only a Western solipsism that regards it as normal to be routinely invading other people's countries in the name of human rights protects NATO governments from serious challenge.

Public Opinion

But the campaign is already coming apart. At home, public opinion is turning against the onslaught: In the US, it's opposed by a margin of two-to-one; in Britain, 43% say they are against the action, compared with 35% in support—an unprecedented level of discontent for the first days of a British military campaign, including Iraq.

On the ground, the Western attacks have failed to halt the fighting and killing, or force Colonel [Muammar] Gaddafi's forces into submission; NATO governments have been squabbling about who's in charge; and British ministers and generals have fallen out about whether the Libyan leader is a legitimate target.

Last week [March 13–19, 2011], NATO governments claimed the support of "the international community" on the back of the UN [United Nations] resolution and an appeal from the dictator-dominated Arab League. In fact, India, Russia, China, Brazil and Germany all refused to support the UN vote and have now criticised or denounced the bombing—as has the African Union and the Arab League itself.

A Step Too Far

As its secretary-general, Amr Moussa, argued, the bombardment clearly went well beyond a no-fly zone from the outset. By attacking regime troops fighting rebel forces on the ground, the NATO governments are unequivocally intervening in a civil war, tilting the balance of forces in favour of the Benghazi-based insurrection.

Cameron insisted on Monday in the Commons [the lower house of British Parliament] that the air and sea attacks on Libya had prevented a "bloody massacre in Benghazi". The main evidence was Gaddafi's threat to show "no mercy" to rebel fighters who refused to lay down their arms and to hunt them down "house to house". In reality, for all the Libyan leader's brutality and [former Iraqi leader] Saddam Hussein-style rhetoric, he was scarcely in any position to carry out his threat.

Given that his ramshackle forces were unable to fully re-take towns like Misrata or even Ajdabiya when the rebels were on the back foot, the idea that they would have been able to overrun an armed and hostile city of 700,000 people any time soon seems far-fetched.

What About Bahrain?

But on the other side of the Arab world, in Western-armed Bahrain, security forces are right now staging night raids on opposition activists, house by house, and scores have gone missing as the dynastic despots carry out a bloody crackdown on the democratic movement. And last Friday more than 50 peaceful demonstrators were shot dead on the streets of Sana'a by government forces in Western-backed Yemen.

Far from imposing a no-fly zone to bring the embattled Yemeni regime to heel, US special forces are operating across the country in support of the government. But then US, British and other NATO forces are themselves responsible for hundreds of thousands of dead in Iraq and Afghanistan. Last week more than 40 civilians were killed by a US drone attack in Pakistan, while over 60 died last month in one US air attack in Afghanistan.

The Hypocrisy of International Intervention

The point isn't just that Western intervention in Libya is grossly hypocritical. It's that such double standards are an integral part of a mechanism of global power and domination that stifles hopes of any credible international system of human rights protection.

À la carte humanitarian intervention, such as in Libya, is certainly not based on feasibility or the degree of suffering or repression, but on whether the regime carrying it out is a reliable ally or not. That's why the claim that Arab despots will be less keen to follow Gaddafi's repressive example as a result of the NATO intervention is entirely unfounded. States such as Saudi Arabia know very well they're not at the slightest risk of being targeted unless they're in danger of collapse.

There's also every chance that, as in Kosovo in 1999, the attack on Libya could actually increase repression and killing, while failing to resolve the underlying conflict. It's scarcely surprising that, outgunned by Gaddafi's forces, the Libyan rebel leadership should be grateful for foreign military support. But any Arab opposition movement that comes to power courtesy of Tornadoes and Tomahawks will be fatally compromised, as would the independence of the country itself.

The Right Side of History

For the Western powers, knocked off balance by the revolutionary Arab tide, intervention in the Libyan conflict offers both the chance to put themselves on the "right side of history" and to secure their oil interests in a deeply uncertain environment.

Unless the Libyan autocrat is assassinated or his regime implodes, the prospect must now be of a bloody stalemate and a Kurdistan-style NATO protectorate in the east. There's little sympathy for Gaddafi in the Arab world, but already influential figures such as the Lebanese Hezbollah leader Hassan Nasrallah have denounced the intervention as a return to the "days of occupation, colonisation and partition".

The urgent alternative is now for countries such as Egypt and Turkey, with a far more legitimate interest in what goes on in Libya and links to all sides, to take the lead in seeking a genuine cease-fire, an end to outside interference and a negotiated political settlement. There is nothing moral about the NATO intervention in Libya—it is a threat to the entire region and its people.

Periodical and Internet Sources Bibliography

The following articles have been selected to supplement the diverse views presented in this chapter.

Simon Adams	"R2P and the Libya Mission," *Los Angeles Times*, September 28, 2011.
M.K. Bhadrakumar	"NATO's Libyan Intervention Evokes Collective Memory of Colonial Era," Global Research, September 6, 2011. http://globalresearch.ca.
David Clark	"Libyan Intervention Was a Success, Despite the Aftermath's Atrocities," *Guardian* (UK), October 28, 2011.
David N. Gibbs	"Power Politics, NATO, and the Libyan Intervention," *Counterpunch*, September 15, 2011.
Gurmeet Kanwal	"Why Intervention in Libya Is Justified," *Economic Times*, April 23, 2011.
Marc Lynch	"What the Libyan Intervention Achieved," *Foreign Policy*, October 27, 2011.
Meghan L. O'Sullivan	"Kurds May Lead the Way for the Arab Spring," Bloomberg.com, June 16, 2011.
Khaled Yacoub Oweis	"Mideast Power Brokers Call for 'Marshall Plan' After Unrest," Reuters, October 22, 2011. www.reuters.com.
Kevin Rudd	"Keep the Faith with the Arab Spring," *Australian*, May 20, 2011.
Ann-Marie Slaughter	"Intervention, Libya, and the Future of Sovereignty," *Atlantic*, September 4, 2011.

OPPOSING
VIEWPOINTS®
SERIES

How Should the United States Respond to the Arab Spring?

Chapter Preface

On February 17, 2011, a revolution was sparked in Libya, an oil-rich country situated on the north coast of Africa. Inspired by popular uprisings in the neighboring countries of Tunisia and Egypt, great numbers of Libyans rose up to depose the country's brutal dictator, Muammar Gaddafi, who had reigned for forty-two years. The uprising in Libya initially began in the city of Benghazi and quickly spread to the nation's capital, Tripoli. Gaddafi, however, was not willing to give up power without a bloody flight. He had encountered opposition many times in his long reign, and he had always ruthlessly quelled it. Up to this point, Gaddafi had always held on to power.

Muammar Gaddafi was born in 1942 in the desert town of Sirte. He came from a family of Bedouins, an ancient tribe of nomadic, desert-dwelling people. From a young age, Gaddafi was a leader. He graduated with honors from the University of Libya, excelled as a member of the Libyan military, and successfully implemented a political coup against Libyan King Idris I in 1969. By age twenty-seven, Gaddafi had become the leader of Libya. He ruled as a military dictator, positioning key military allies and cronies in important roles. For years, he supported terrorist efforts in countries around the world, including Chad, the Philippines, Northern Ireland, Liberia, and Iran. In 2003 Gaddafi admitted his role in supporting the two Libyan terrorists who planted a bomb on Pan Am Flight 103, which blew up over Lockerbie, Scotland, killing 270 people in 1988.

Gaddafi was considered thoroughly corrupt and brutal by the Libyan people. He appointed family and friends in government and business, allowing them to enrich themselves at the expense of others. Civic organizing or expression often resulted in violent crackdowns and imprisonment. Income disparity grew, as Gaddafi and his cronies got richer and the rest of the country got poorer, despite the nation's wealth from the oil business. Gaddafi exhibited eccentric behavior, surrounding himself with a cadre of beautiful female bodyguards. He dressed in flamboyant outfits and made bizarre pronouncements. The press nicknamed him "The Mad Dog of the Middle East."

As the Arab Spring spread to Libya in February 2011, Gaddafi met protests with aggressive violence. Security forces shot randomly into crowds. Snipers took out protest leaders. Foreign mercenaries were brought in to mercilessly beat and shoot protesters. Helicopters hovered over crowds and snipers sprayed bullets to kill and spread panic. For protesters, there was no turning back. They organized into an opposition army to finally overthrow Gaddafi. If Gaddafi got the upper hand, international observers speculated that he would mercilessly slaughter thousands of protesters and opposition fighters.

By March 2011, the international community had decided to intervene in the Libyan civil war by providing much-needed assistance to rebel forces. On March 17, 2011, the United Nations Security Council adopted Resolution 1973, which called for immediate intervention in the conflict.

In the United States, intervention in Libya provoked a storm of controversy. Many people did not want the country to get involved in another war when the United States still had troops in Iraq and Afghanistan. Some congressional leaders complained that Congress wasn't properly consulted before the use of force in Libya. A number of Republican and Democratic leaders argued that President Barack Obama's actions were unconstitutional because the president does not have the right to authorize military action without the consent of Congress.

Despite the controversy, international efforts to help the rebel forces in Libya commenced. The North Atlantic Treaty Organization (NATO) established a no-fly zone over much of

Libya and provided air strikes against Gaddafi forces. In late August, rebel troops gained control over Tripoli, and Gaddafi and his family went into hiding. His reign as despot in Libya was over. As President Obama noted at that time, "For over four decades, the Libyan people have lived under the rule of a tyrant who denied them their most basic human rights. Now, the celebrations that we've seen in the streets of Libya show that the pursuit of human dignity is far stronger than any dictator."

On October 20, 2011, Gaddafi, hiding near his hometown of Sirte, was caught by rebel forces; he was brutally killed and his bloody corpse put on display.

The debate over US intervention in Libya is one of the issues covered in the following chapter, which explores how the US should respond to the Arab Spring. Other viewpoints in the chapter examine America's support for Middle East dictators as well as democratic reform and foreign aid to the region.

> "We have embraced the chance to show that America values the dignity of the street vendor in Tunisia more than the raw power of the dictator."

The United States Should Support Democratic Movements in the Middle East

Barack Obama

Barack Obama is the forty-fourth president of the United States. In the following viewpoint, he claims that the United States has an important opportunity to stand with the protesters of the Arab Spring and support their call for self-determination and greater opportunity. President Obama argues that America must proceed with a sense of humility and continue to oppose the use of violence and repression against the protesters. Moreover, he points out that America must make the changes happening in the Middle East and North Africa a top priority and support the protesters with all the diplomatic, economic, and strategic tools at the government's disposal.

As you read, consider the following questions:

1. What al Qaeda leader's death does President Obama identify as a huge blow to the terrorist organization?

Barack Obama, "A Moment of Opportunity," WhiteHouse.gov, May 19, 2011.

2. According to President Obama, what event in Tunisia sparked the Arab Spring?

3. What rights does President Obama consider as universal?

The State Department is a fitting venue to mark a new chapter in American diplomacy. For six months, we have witnessed an extraordinary change take place in the Middle East and North Africa. Square by square, town by town, country by country, the people have risen up to demand their basic human rights. Two leaders have stepped aside. More may follow. And though these countries may be a great distance from our shores, we know that our own future is bound to this region by the forces of economics and security, history and faith.

Today [May 19, 2011] I would like to talk about this change—the forces that are driving it, and how we can respond in a way that advances our values and strengthens our security. Already we have done much to shift our foreign policy following a decade defined by two costly conflicts. After years of war in Iraq, we have removed 100,000 American troops and ended our combat mission there. In Afghanistan we have broken the Taliban's momentum, and this July we will begin to bring our troops home and continue transition to Afghan lead. And after years of war against al-Qaida and its affiliates, we have dealt al-Qaida a huge blow by killing its leader, Osama bin Laden.

Osama bin Laden and Al-Qaida

Bin Laden was no martyr. He was a mass murderer who offered a message of hate—an insistence that Muslims had to take up arms against the West, and that violence against men, women and children was the only path to change. He rejected democracy and individual rights for Muslims in favor of violent extremism; his agenda focused on what he could destroy—not what he could build.

Bin Laden and his murderous vision won some adherents. But even before his death, al-Qaida was losing its struggle for relevance, as the overwhelming majority of people saw that the slaughter of innocents did not answer their cries for a better life. By the time we found bin Laden, al-Qaida's agenda had come to be seen by the vast majority of the region as a dead end, and the people of the Middle East and North Africa had taken their future into their own hands.

The Arab Spring

That story of self-determination began six months ago in Tunisia. On Dec. 17 [2010] a young vendor named Mohamed Bouazizi was devastated when a police officer confiscated his cart. This was not unique. It is the same kind of humiliation that takes place every day in many parts of the world—the relentless tyranny of governments that deny their citizens dignity. Only this time, something different happened. After local officials refused to hear his complaint, this young man who had never been particularly active in politics went to the headquarters of the provincial government, doused himself in fuel and lit himself on fire.

Sometimes, in the course of history, the actions of ordinary citizens spark movements for change because they speak to a longing for freedom that has built up for years. In America, think of the defiance of those patriots in Boston who refused to pay taxes to a king, or the dignity of Rosa Parks as she sat courageously in her seat. So it was in Tunisia, as that vendor's act of desperation tapped into the frustration felt throughout the country. Hundreds of protesters took to the streets, then thousands. And in the face of batons and sometimes bullets, they refused to go home—day after day, week after week, until a dictator of more than two decades finally left power.

Fighting for the Right to Self-Determination

The story of this revolution, and the ones that followed, should not have come as a surprise. The nations of the Middle East and North Africa won their independence long ago, but in too many places their people did not. In too many countries, power has been concentrated in the hands of the few. In too many countries, a citizen like that young vendor had nowhere to turn—no honest judiciary to hear his case; no independent media to give him voice; no credible political party to represent his views; no free and fair election where he could choose his leader.

This lack of self-determination—the chance to make of your life what you will—has applied to the region's economy as well. Yes, some nations are blessed with wealth in oil and gas, and that has led to pockets of prosperity. But in a global economy based on knowledge and innovation, no development strategy can be based solely upon what comes out of the ground. Nor can people reach their potential when you cannot start a business without paying a bribe.

Time for Change

In the face of these challenges, too many leaders in the region tried to direct their people's grievances elsewhere. The West was blamed as the source of all ills, a half century after the end of colonialism. Antagonism toward Israel became the only acceptable outlet for political expression. Divisions of tribe, ethnicity and religious sect were manipulated as a means of holding on to power or taking it away from somebody else.

But the events of the past six months show us that strategies of repression and diversion won't work anymore. Satellite television and the Internet provide a window into the wider world—a world of astonishing progress in places like India, Indonesia and Brazil. Cell phones and social networks allow young people to connect and organize like never before. A new generation has emerged. And their voices tell us that change cannot be denied.

In Cairo we heard the voice of the young mother who said, "It's like I can finally breathe fresh air for the first time."

In Sana'a we heard the students who chanted, "The night must come to an end."

In Benghazi we heard the engineer who said, "Our words are free now. It's a feeling you can't explain."

In Damascus we heard the young man who said, "After the first yelling, the first shout, you feel dignity."

Those shouts of human dignity are being heard across the region. And through the moral force of nonviolence, the people of the region have achieved more change in six months than terrorists have accomplished in decades.

America's Role in the Arab Spring

Of course, change of this magnitude does not come easily. In our day and age—a time of 24-hour news cycles, and constant communication—people expect the transformation of the region to be resolved in a matter of weeks. But it will be years before this story reaches its end. Along the way, there will be good days, and bad days. In some places, change will be swift; in others, gradual. And as we have seen, calls for change may give way to fierce contests for power.

The question before us is what role America will play as this story unfolds. For decades the United States has pursued a set of core interests in the region: countering terrorism and stopping the spread of nuclear weapons; securing the free flow of commerce and safeguarding the security of the region; standing up for Israel's security and pursuing Arab-Israeli peace.

President Barack Obama's 2009 Cairo Speech

I have come here to seek a new beginning between the United States and Muslims around the world; one based upon mutual interest and mutual respect; and one based upon the truth that America and Islam are not exclusive, and need not be in competition. Instead, they overlap, and share common principles—principles of justice and progress; tolerance and the dignity of all human beings.

I do so recognizing that change cannot happen overnight. No single speech can eradicate years of mistrust, nor can I answer in the time that I have all the complex questions that brought us to this point. But I am convinced that in order to move forward, we must say openly the things we hold in our hearts, and that too often are said only behind closed doors. There must be a sustained effort to listen to each other; to learn from each other; to respect one another; and to seek common ground. As the Holy Koran tells us, "Be conscious of God and speak always the truth." That is what I will try to do—to speak the truth as best I can, humbled by the task before us, and firm in my belief that the interests we share as human beings are far more powerful than the forces that drive us apart.

Barack Obama, "A New Beginning," speech, Cairo University, Egypt, June 4, 2009.

We will continue to do these things, with the firm belief that America's interests are not hostile to people's hopes; they are essential to them. We believe that no one benefits from a nuclear arms race in the region, or al-Qaida's brutal attacks. People everywhere would see their economies crippled by a cut off in energy supplies. As we did in the Gulf War, we will not tolerate aggression across borders, and we will keep our commitments to friends and partners.

Yet we must acknowledge that a strategy based solely upon the narrow pursuit of these interests will not fill an empty stomach or allow someone to speak their mind. Moreover, failure to speak to the broader aspirations of ordinary people will only feed the suspicion that has festered for years that the United States pursues our own interests at their expense. Given that this mistrust runs both ways—as Americans have been seared by hostage taking, violent rhetoric and terrorist attacks that have killed thousands of our citizens—a failure to change our approach threatens a deepening spiral of division between the United States and Muslim communities.

That's why, two years ago in Cairo, I began to broaden our engagement based upon mutual interests and mutual respect. I believed then—and I believe now—that we have a stake not just in the stability of nations, but in the self-determination of individuals. The status quo is not sustainable. Societies held together by fear and repression may offer the illusion of stability for a time, but they are built upon fault lines that will eventually tear asunder.

The United States Must Welcome Change

So we face a historic opportunity. We have embraced the chance to show that America values the dignity of the street vendor in Tunisia more than the raw power of the dictator. There must be no doubt that the United States of America welcomes change that advances self-determination and opportunity. Yes, there will be perils that accompany this moment of promise. But after decades of accepting the world as it is in the region, we have a chance to pursue the world as it should be.

As we do, we must proceed with a sense of humility. It is not America that put people into the streets of Tunis and

Cairo—it was the people themselves who launched these movements and must determine their outcome. Not every country will follow our particular form of representative democracy, and there will be times when our short-term interests do not align perfectly with our long-term vision of the region. But we can—and will—speak out for a set of core principles—principles that have guided our response to the events over the past six months.

The United States opposes the use of violence and repression against the people of the region.

A Top Priority

We support a set of universal rights. Those rights include free speech; the freedom of peaceful assembly; freedom of religion; equality for men and women under the rule of law; and the right to choose your own leaders—whether you live in Baghdad or Damascus, Sana'a or Tehran.

And finally, we support political and economic reform in the Middle East and North Africa that can meet the legitimate aspirations of ordinary people throughout the region.

Our support for these principles is not a secondary interest. Today I am making it clear that it is a top priority that must be translated into concrete actions and supported by all of the diplomatic, economic and strategic tools at our disposal.

> "Since 2009, [the President Barack Obama administration has] sought to arm some of the most antidemocratic regimes on the planet, while repeatedly highlighting the need for democratic reform and now for a fresh start in the region."

The United States Should Not Continue to Support Middle East Dictators

Nick Turse

Nick Turse is an investigative journalist and the associate editor of TomDispatch.com. In the following viewpoint, he points out that while the administration of President Barack Obama is talking about supporting the changes in the Middle East and North Africa and standing with the protesters' calls for self-determination and justice, it has been selling billions of dollars of high-tech weapons and equipment to repressive regimes in the region. In fact, many of the weapons sold by the United States are then being used against the very protesters President Obama claims to support. Turse argues that if Obama wants his rhetoric to match his actions, he must stand up to the US military-industrial complex, particularly the Department of Defense.

As you read, consider the following questions:

1. According to the author, what did Egypt's military recently receive from the Pentagon?

2. According to a 2010 Congressional Research Service report, what percentage of all arms agreements with Middle Eastern nations were with the United States from 2006 to 2009?

3. How much money does the author say that the six member states of the Gulf Cooperation Council are going to spend on American weaponry and equipment in 2011?

If you follow the words, one Middle East comes into view; if you follow the weapons, quite another.

This week [in May 2011], the words will take center stage. On Thursday, according to administration officials, President [Barack] Obama will "reset" American policy in the Middle East with a major address offering a comprehensive look at the Arab Spring, "a unified theory about the popular uprisings from Tunisia to Bahrain," and possibly a new administration approach to the region.

In the meantime, all signs indicate that the Pentagon will quietly maintain antithetical policies, just as it has throughout the Obama years. Barring an unprecedented and almost inconceivable policy shift, it will continue to broker lucrative deals to send weapons systems and military equipment to Arab despots. Nothing indicates that it will be deterred from its course, whatever the president says, which means that Barack Obama's reset rhetoric is unlikely to translate into meaningful policy change in the region.

The Arab Spring

For months now, the world has watched as protesters have taken to the streets across the Middle East to demand a greater say in their lives. In Tunisia and Egypt, they toppled decades-old dictatorships. In Bahrain and Yemen, they were shot down in the streets as they demanded democracy. In the United Arab Emirates, Kuwait, Jordan and Saudi Arabia, they called for reforms, free speech, and basic rights, and ended up bloodied and often in jail cells. In Iraq, they protested a lack of food and jobs, and in response got bullets and beatings.

As the world watched, trained eyes couldn't help noticing something startling about the tools of repression in those countries. The armored personnel carriers, tanks, and helicopters used to intimidate or even kill peaceful protesters were often American models.

The U.S. Role in Repressive Arab Regimes

For decades, the U.S. has provided military aid, facilitated the sale of weaponry, and transferred vast quantities of arms to a host of Middle Eastern despots. Arming Arab autocrats, however, isn't only the work of presidents past. A TomDispatch analysis of Pentagon documents finds that the Obama administration has sought to send billions of dollars in weapons systems—from advanced helicopters to fighter jets—to the very regimes that have beaten, jailed, and killed pro-democracy demonstrators, journalists, and reform activists throughout the Arab Spring.

The administration's abiding support for the militaries of repressive regimes calls into question the president's rhetoric about change. The arms deals of recent years also shed light on the shadowy, mutually supportive relationships among the U.S. military, top arms dealers, and Arab states that are of increasing importance to the Pentagon.

Since the summer of 2009, President Obama, by way of the Pentagon and with State Department approval, has regularly notified Congress of his intent to sell advanced weaponry to governments across the Middle East, including Bahrain, Egypt, Iraq, Jordan, Kuwait, Saudi Arabia, Tunisia, and the United Arab Emirates (UAE). Under U.S. law, Congress then has 30 days to review the sale before the Pentagon and associated military contractors enter into more formal contract talks with individual nations.

New Business

In July 2009, according to an analysis of Pentagon documents by TomDispatch, notifications were sent to Congress regarding the sale to Kuwait of Browning machine guns, advanced targeting systems for armored vehicles, KC-130 aircraft, and technical support for F/A-18 attack aircraft. Later that summer, the White House announced plans to outfit both Bahrain's and Jordan's militaries with advanced air-to-air missiles to the tune of $74 million and $131 million, respectively, to equip the United Arab Emirates with $526 million worth of Hellfire missiles and other materiel, to send more than $2 billion worth of advanced surveillance and navigation equipment to aid Saudi Arabia's air force, and to see to it that Egypt's military received a shipment of new Chinook troop transport helicopters and other high-tech equipment valued at $308 million.

In the fall of 2009, Pentagon documents show a $220 million bid by the administration to outfit the Jordanian military with advanced rocket systems and tactical vehicles; a proposed sale of advanced fighter aircraft, parts, weapons, and equipment to Egypt worth as much as $3.2 billion; and another to equip Kuwait's military with $410 million in Patriot missile technology. Then, in November and December of that year, Congress was notified of plans to sell helicopters to Iraq; Javelin guided missiles to Jordan; Hellfire missiles, anti-ship cruise missiles, jet engines, and other military materiel to Egypt; and helicopters and thousands of advanced bombs, among other high-tech equipment, to the UAE.

Last year, notifications also went out concerning the sale of F-16 fighters, armored personnel carriers, tank ammunition, and advanced computer systems to Iraq; C-17 military transport aircraft for Kuwait; mobile missile systems for Bahrain; and Apache attack helicopters and tactical missile systems for the United Arab Emirates. Saudi Arabia, however, was the big winner by far with a blockbuster $60 billion agreement for helicopters, fighter jets, radar equipment, and advanced smart bombs that will represent, if all purchases are made, the largest foreign arms deal in American history.

Deficits, Ducats, and Dictators

The agreement to broker the sale of tens of billions of dollars worth of weapons to Saudi Arabia sheds light on the Pentagon's efforts to shield itself—and its favored arms dealers—from the shakiness of the American economy, as well as President Obama's stated goal of trimming $400 billion from projected national security spending of $10 trillion over the next 12 years. Last October, the Pentagon started secretly lobbying financial analysts and large institutional investors on behalf of weapons makers and other military contractors. The idea was to bolster their long-term financial viability in the face of a possible future slowdown in Defense Department spending.

Since then, Deputy Secretary of Defense William Lynn and other Pentagon power brokers have made regular trips to New York City to shore up Wall Street's support for weapons manufacturers. "We are in this for the long term. We need industrial partners and financial backers who think and act likewise," Lynn told investors at a recent defense and aerospace conference in that city.

Along with Ashton Carter, the Pentagon's undersecretary of defense for acquisition, technology, and logistics, and Brett

Lambert, the deputy assistant secretary for industrial policy, Lynn is creating a comprehensive plan to sustain and enrich weapons makers and other military contractors in the coming years. "We're going sector by sector, tier by tier, and our goal is to develop a long-term policy to protect that base as we slow defense spending," Lynn said. America's Middle Eastern allies are seen as a significant partner in this effort.

It's often said that the Pentagon is a "monopsony"—that is, the only buyer in town for its many giant contractors. As has been amply demonstrated since Barack Obama took office, however, it's not true. When it comes to the Middle East, the Pentagon acts not as a buyer, but as a broker and shill, clearing the way for its Middle Eastern partners to buy some of the world's most advanced weaponry.

A Booming Trade

And Arab allies have distinctly done their part for the Pentagon. From 2006 to 2009, according to a report by the Congressional Research Service issued late last year, the United States accounted for 52.4% of all arms agreements inked with Middle Eastern nations—to the tune of $47.3 billion. (By comparison, the United Kingdom, in second place in arms sales in the region, accounted for only 15.7% and third-place Russia just 12.8%.)

The purchases of the chief buyer in the Middle East, Saudi Arabia, have been climbing steadily. From 2002 to 2005, Saudi Arabia inked $15.3 billion in arms-transfer agreements with the United States. From 2006 to 2009, that figure jumped to $29.5 billion. The multiyear $60 billion deal in 2010 signaled far more of the same and will help ensure the continuing health and profitability of Boeing, Lockheed Martin, and other mega-defense contractors even if Pentagon spending goes slack or begins to shrink in the years to come.

The Call for an Arms Trade Treaty (ATT)

All across the [Middle East and North Africa (MENA)] region, government authorities responded to protests seen as heralding an "Arab Spring" by using excessive, often lethal force even against peaceful demonstrators while deploying a wide range of weaponry, munitions, armaments and related materiel much of it imported from abroad. In Bahrain, Egypt and Yemen, riot police and internal security forces used firearms, shotguns and shotgun cartridges, live ammunition, rubber bullets, tear gas, water cannons and armoured vehicles to suppress and disperse protesters. In Libya, as the country slid into armed conflict, Colonel Mu'ammar al-Gaddafi's forces launched Grad rockets, mortars and fired artillery into densely populated civilian residential areas. In Syria too, government forces have used heavy weaponry, artillery and tanks to fire at civilian areas in their efforts to crush the protests. Incredibly, however, thousands upon thousands of ordinary people have maintained their protests and refused to be cowed by high levels of state violence.

The protests have brought sharply into focus the appalling human rights records of many governments in the MENA region, which Amnesty International has been documenting for decades. They have also highlighted how the sale and supply of weaponry, munitions and related equipment to those very same governments have impacted on human rights in the region. Used against protesters, the majority of this weaponry, munitions and related equipment was sold and supplied by European countries, Russia and the USA.

"Arms Transfers to the Middle East and North Africa: Lessons for an Effective Arms Trade Treaty," Amnesty International, 2011.

Follow the Money

The Pentagon's reliance on the deep pockets of Arab partners across the Middle East, however, has a price, which may help to explain the Obama administration's willingness to support dictators like Tunisia's Zine El Abidine Ben Ali and Egypt's Hosni Mubarak until their ousters were givens, and to essentially look the other way as security forces in Bahrain, Saudi Arabia, Yemen, and elsewhere, sometimes using American-supplied equipment, suppressed pro-democracy activists. After all, the six member states of the Gulf Cooperation Council [also known as the Cooperation Council for the Arab States of the Gulf]—Bahrain, Kuwait, Oman, Qatar, Saudi Arabia, and the UAE, along with regional partner Jordan—are set to spend $70 billion on American weaponry and equipment this year, and as much as $80 billion per year by 2015.

"The Middle East Military Air Market: Revenue Opportunities and Stakeholder Mapping," a recent analysis of just one sector of defense spending in the region by U.S.-based defense consultants Frost & Sullivan, projects yet more growth in the future. "[The] regional military air market is . . . set to generate revenues of $62.9 billion between 2010 and 2020," it reports. Frost & Sullivan analysts add that Saudi Arabia and the United Arab Emirates are likely to be the biggest spenders and will continue to buy most of their arms through the United States for the sake of "political influence."

For his part, Deputy Secretary of Defense Lynn wants to make it ever easier to put sophisticated military technology in the hands of such deep-pocketed allies. On his recent trip to New York, he spoke of streamlining the process by which tanks, jets, and other advanced weapons systems are sold around the world. "To keep our base healthy, it is in our interest for defense companies to compete globally," he explained, while deriding the current system for selling arms abroad as "archaic" and in need of an overhaul. "The barriers that we place at this point in the export control system look something like a marriage of the complexity of the Internal Revenue Service with the efficiency of the Department of Motor Vehicles," he said. "It's something we have to change."

Sending a Message

In February, in Baghdad, Fallujah, Mosul, and Tikrit, Iraqi protesters took to the streets, focused on ending corruption and chronic shortages of food, water, electricity, and jobs. In response, Prime Minister Nouri al-Maliki, who has in recent years consolidated power with U.S. military backing, unleashed government security forces. They arrested, beat, and shot protesters, leaving hundreds dead or wounded. In the weeks since, the Obama administration has not only failed to forcefully rebuke the Maliki regime, but has announced its intent to bolster those same security forces with another $360 million in military materiel ranging from radios to radar systems.

In March, the United Arab Emirates [UAE] sent security forces into neighboring Bahrain to help put down pro-democracy protests. Early the next month, UAE security forces [detained] leading human rights activist Ahmed Mansoor and, in the days thereafter, detained at least four other prominent democracy activists. Before the month was out, however, the Obama administration announced its intention to arm the UAE with advanced Sidewinder tactical missiles.

Saudi Arabia also sent troops into Bahrain and has been cracking down on nonviolent activists at home with increasing vigor. At the beginning of this month, for example, Human Rights Watch reported the arrest of "at least 20 peaceful protesters, including two bloggers." Within days, the Obama administration notified Congress of its intent to see the Saudi security forces receive $330 million worth of advanced night vision and thermal imaging equipment.

This year, U.S.-coordinated arms sales have resulted in the delivery of helicopter gunships to Yemen, navy patrol boats to Iraq, and the first of six cargo aircraft to the UAE. At the moment, used armored personnel carriers are being refurbished for shipment to Iraq later this year.

U.S. Hypocrisy

Whatever "reset" may be in the works for Obama administration policies in the Middle East, the president and the Pentagon are already on the record. Since 2009, they have sought to arm some of the most antidemocratic regimes on the planet, while repeatedly highlighting the need for democratic reform and now for a fresh start in the region. Even as the "reset" begins, the Pentagon is leaning ever more heavily on rich rulers in the Arab world to prop up the military-corporate complex at home. If the Pentagon and the weapons makers have their way, the provisional successes of the demonstrators in Egypt and Tunisia will turn out to be outliers as an Arab Spring turns distinctly wintry.

In June 2009, President Obama traveled to Cairo University to give a heavily hyped and much-lauded speech. . . . In his remarks, the president spoke of an American Cold War–era attitude "in which Muslim-majority countries were too often treated as proxies without regard to their own aspirations." Then came his first call for a reset of sorts in the region. "I've come here to Cairo," he said, "to seek a new beginning between the United States and Muslims around the world, one based on mutual interest and mutual respect." Before that summer was out, however, Obama notified Congress of his intent to send Cold War–era autocrat Hosni Mubarak a shipment of new helicopters to beef up his security forces.

During that speech, Obama talked of his "unyielding belief" that all people yearned for free speech, a say in their governance, the rule of law, freedom from corruption, and other basic civil liberties. These weren't, the president insisted, just American ideals, they were human rights. "And that is why we will support them everywhere," he said to waves of applause.

In its actions, however, the Obama administration almost immediately left its reset rhetoric in the dust. Whether the president does any better in the Arab Summer of 2011 will depend mightily on whether he can stand up to the Pentagon and its weapons makers.

> "Intervention into a country's internal
> affairs, as last decade taught us the
> hard way, can have grave unintended
> consequences."

The United States Should Refrain from Intervening in the Middle East

Matt Welch

Matt Welch is editor in chief of Reason. *In the following viewpoint, he asserts that America should welcome its diminishing role in the Middle East and North Africa. Welch points out that change in the Arab world should come from the grassroots level, arguing that it will have a better chance to succeed and benefit the people than if it comes from an outside power. He states that the United States has learned from the war in Iraq that it is best to take a backseat when it comes to similar situations.*

As you read, consider the following questions:

1. What event does the author think turned the tide against Hosni Mubarak in Egypt, who was eventually forced from office?

2. According to the author, how much did the Muammar Qaddafi regime pay the PR firm Monitor Group to burnish Libya's image?

3. Who does Welch say Senator John McCain designated as the hero in Tunisia?

In October 2010, best-selling *New Yorker* essayist Malcolm Gladwell published a piece titled "Small Change: Why the Revolution Will Not Be Tweeted," a derisive attack on the notion that social networking websites would ever play a major role in fomenting meaningful nonviolent resistance to authoritarian regimes. "If you're taking on a powerful and organized establishment you have to be a hierarchy," Gladwell argued. "Think of the ceaseless pattern of correction and revision, amendment and debate, that characterizes Wikipedia. If Martin Luther King, Jr., had tried to do a wiki-boycott in Montgomery, he would have been steamrollered by the white power structure."

Less than six months later, a series of mostly nonviolent and nonhierarchical protests drove longtime Egyptian dictator Hosni Mubarak out of office, part of a transnational wave of pro-liberalization protest that is remaking North Africa and the Middle East. One of the most influential Egyptian activists was a young Google executive named Wael Ghonim. The tide arguably turned against Mubarak when he tried to shut down the Internet. "Our revolution," Ghonim told *60 Minutes*, "is like Wikipedia, OK?"

Libya's Public Relations Push

Gladwell was not the only deep thinker rendered ridiculous by the remarkable events of early 2011. In mid-January, controversial commentator Stephen M. Walt wrote a confident prediction in a *Foreign Policy* article titled "Why the Tunisian Revolution Won't Spread." And in March, as the increasingly deranged Libyan leader Col. Muammar al-Qaddafi sent his warplanes to strafe unarmed protesters even while denying that there *were* any anti-regime demonstrations (let alone whole swaths of the country under rebel control), *Mother Jones* and other outlets began excavating a trove of embarrassing op-ed pieces published in 2007 by intellectuals who swore that Qaddafi had turned over a new leaf. (Many of the Qaddafi enthusiasts failed to disclose that they were on the payroll of the P.R. [public relations] firm Monitor Group, which had taken a $3 million annual contract to burnish Libya's image.)

"Surprisingly flexible and pragmatic, [Qaddafi] was once an ardent socialist who now acknowledges private property and capital as sometimes appropriate elements in developing societies," wrote *Jihad vs. McWorld* author (and Monitor recipient) Benjamin Barber in a typical specimen of the genre, published in the *Washington Post* in August 2007. "Libya under [Qaddafi] has embarked on a journey that could make it the first Arab state to transition peacefully and without overt Western intervention to a stable, non-autocratic government and, in time, to an indigenous mixed constitution favoring direct democracy locally and efficient government centrally."

It wasn't just intellectuals, bought off or not, who were caught off guard by the pro-democracy wave. On January 25, Secretary of State Hillary Clinton characterized the Egyptian government as "stable." On January 30, Clinton was talking about an "orderly transition" lasting months. On Feb. 11, Mubarak resigned, prompting Clinton's boss Barack Obama to say, "Egyptians have made it clear that nothing less than genuine democracy will carry the day."

Lessons Learned

What lessons can we draw from Americans' seeming inability to predict or even process the thrilling and harrowing events of the Arab Spring? First and foremost: It's really not about us—in every sense of the phrase.

Islamist-fearing skeptics of the 2011 revolutions have often invoked the Iranian revolution of 1979. Yet the Great Satan has been almost nowhere to be found on the streets of Cairo, Tripoli, or Sana'a. Whether in an Egypt awash in U.S. foreign aid or a Libya that for decades was under U.S. sanctions, protesters have focused instead on the local guy keeping them down. This is evident not just in the handmade street signs and lack of burning flags but in most of what we know about the intellectual underpinnings of the movement.

In March 2004, a group of civil society leaders from the Middle East and North Africa convened at the fancy new library in Alexandria to sketch out some architecture for the freedom they wanted. The resulting Alexandria declaration, very reminiscent of Czechoslovakia's Charter 77 and copycat dissident documents across the unfree world, was short on complaints about Yankee imperialism and long on demands for enumerated freedoms that until recently sounded like science fiction in an Arab context.

"When we talk of democratic systems, we mean, without ambiguity, genuine democracy," the declaration states. "Democracy is based on respect of all rights for all the people, including freedom of thought and expression, and the right to organize under the umbrella of effective political institutions, with an elected legislature, an independent judiciary, a government that is subject to both constitutional and public accountability, and political parties of different intellectual and ideological orientations. This genuine democracy requires guaranteed freedom of expression in all its forms, topmost among which is freedom of the press, and audio-visual and electronic media."

America's Changing Role in Arab Affairs

You could even detect the balance of power shifting from Uncle Sam to the mythical "Arab street" in the way that embattled authoritarians addressed their own people. Hand-

America's Shifting Position on Egypt

The "Arab Spring" created dramatic contrasts between America's professed ideals and its actual behavior. As the Egyptian crisis heated up, the [President Barack] Obama administration embraced President [Hosni] Mubarak. Then Washington suggested an orderly transition to democracy. Officials next suggested a faster transfer of power. With Mubarak's ouster, the U.S. enthusiastically embraced change. It was a shameless performance that fooled no one.

Doug Bandow,
"A Foreign Policy Fit for a Republic,"
Daily Caller, May 30, 2011.

picked Mubarak successor Omar Suleiman, a day before the dictator's resignation, pointed his finger not at the Obama administration (or even Twitter!) but at Al Jazeera: "Do not listen to the satellite stations that have no objective but to sew sedition among people and to weaken Egypt and to mar its image," Suleiman admonished protesters. He, too, was gone by the end of the week.

The anticommunist resolutions of 1989 taught us that local, ground-up ownership of revolutions, particularly of the nonviolent variety, correlate strongly with post-totalitarian success. Yet judging by the reaction of many American commentators, the non-centrality of Washington's role has come as a disappointment, even a disgrace. "The passivity of the Obama administration has damaged America's interests and standing around the world," *Weekly Standard* editor William Kristol warned. "America should lead," Sen. John McCain (R-Ariz.) said in the middle of a multi-country tour of the region in late February. McCain, whose proposed doctrine of "rogue state rollback" would have required maybe half a dozen military interventions thus far during the Arab Spring, was chagrined that "The No. 1 hero in Tunisia" is not President Obama, but "a guy named Mark Zuckerberg." At a minimum, McCain maintained, we should be enforcing a no-fly zone over Libya.

Washington's secondary-at-best role in this revolutionary moment is a harbinger of things to come. As historian Niall Ferguson aptly framed the issue last year in *Foreign Policy*, "There is a zero-sum game at the heart of the budgetary process: if interest payments consume a rising proportion of tax revenue, military expenditure is the item most likely to be cut because, unlike mandatory entitlements, it is discretionary. . . . U.S. fiscal policy today is preprogrammed to reduce the resources available for all overseas military operations in the years ahead."

A Welcome Transition

An America that is already broke, with unfunded liabilities in the trillions and entitlement trajectories that the president himself has described as "unsustainable" (without doing a damned bit about it), is an America that will no longer be the protagonist in all the world's dramas. This, I believe, is a welcome and long-overdue development. But it won't be easy, or clean.

Freedom is messy. Attempted revolutions in regions that haven't experienced liberalism are guaranteed to have terrifying moments, even decades. The analogical revolutionary year might be less 1989, more 1848. And 1848 didn't end up well for most revolutionaries [referring to a series of revolutions throughout Europe in which the uprisings were unsuccessful]. Although it is horrible on a basic human level to watch impotently from afar as a delusional thug mows down his own people, that does not mean the U.S. or the international community can produce the best long- or even short-term outcome for the country. Intervention into a country's internal affairs, as last decade taught us the hard way, can have grave unintended consequences.

With America as a bystander, on the other hand, protesters and rebels are seizing the means of democratic production. They are taking ownership of their own future. It's time that we let them.

> *"Our most useful contribution now would be to strengthen reform and reformers by conditioning every cent of aid."*

The United States Needs to Make Aid to Arab Countries Conditional

Elliott Abrams

Elliott Abrams is a senior fellow at the Council on Foreign Relations and the former deputy national security advisor for global democracy strategy under the George W. Bush administration. In the following viewpoint, he maintains that the United States should condition aid to some of the countries in the Arab world in order to pressure corrupt and repressive leaders to enact significant electoral, political, and economic reforms. Abrams argues that by handing over money with no conditions the United States is allowing countries to avoid reform. Aid must be tied to reform, benchmarks must be clear and strict, and there must be consequences if regimes do not meet the goal, Abrams insists.

As you read, consider the following questions:

1. According to Abrams, what kind of dynasty rules in Bahrain?

2. How much does Abrams say the Saudi king gave away in subsidies in March 2011?

3. In what countries does the author believe that the United States can have some leverage over the pace of reform?

The fake republics are goners; the monarchies have a fighting chance. That's my conclusion after a short visit to the Middle East and discussions with officials and analysts there.

The ingredients that brought [Zine El Abidine] Ben Ali down in Tunisia were closely replicated in Egypt and Libya: repression, vast corruption, and family rule. They are all present in Syria as well, suggesting that the [Bashar al-]Assad regime may stay in power for a while by shooting protesting citizens, but that its ultimate demise is certain.

The monarchies, especially Jordan and Morocco, have some genuine legitimacy, as do the Gulf states as well. They are less repressive and more legitimate than the now-overthrown false republics, with their stolen elections, regime-dominated courts, and rubber-stamp parliaments. Unlike the republics of fear, these monarchies do not have histories of bloody repression and jails filled with political prisoners. (Bahrain is an exception, for the Sunni dynasty ruling over a Shia population always had less legitimacy—and may now have fatally compromised whatever was left of it by bringing in Saudi and other foreign troops to crush demonstrations.)

Meanwhile, the Saudi crackdown on Shia protesters in Bahrain has surely angered the Saudis' own Shia in the oil-rich Eastern Province. They live in a country owned by a Sunni dynasty that hates and fears them. The instability in Bahrain is rightly viewed by the Saudi royals as dangerous, but their actions have made it far worse and far more likely to have repercussions for them at home.

The Role of the United States

What can the United States do? We have little leverage over the oil-rich Saudis, Emiratis, and Qataris, who appear in the last year or two to have lost all faith that Washington has anything of value to tell them. But we do have influence elsewhere, in Jordan and Morocco, and in Egypt and Tunisia, all aid recipients. Our most useful contribution now would be to strengthen reform and reformers by conditioning every cent of aid. Our security-based largesse to Egypt and Jordan during the Iraq War allowed them to avoid reform and meant that reformers had less clout. And the tight military-to-military and intelligence relationships also reduced pressure for reform—not only in the region but in Washington as well. "All that money you threw at us killed reform," a Jordanian official told me, "and our security guys told the king he didn't need to do anything." The key now is to apply to all our assistance the approach that some of it gets through the Millennium Challenge Corporation, where aid is tied tightly to reform, benchmarks are strict, and assistance is reduced or ended for nonperformance.

The Need for Reform

The question for the kings, emirs, and sheiks is whether they will do two things: end the corruption that surrounds all these royal courts, and begin a genuine move toward constitutional monarchy, where power is shared between the throne and the people. In Kuwait there is already a real, elected parliament with genuine power, but the prime minister is always a member of the ruling al-Sabah family. That must end.

In Jordan, where the prime minister is always a commoner, the king has announced some new reforms that would tend to move the country toward a more democratic system: notably,

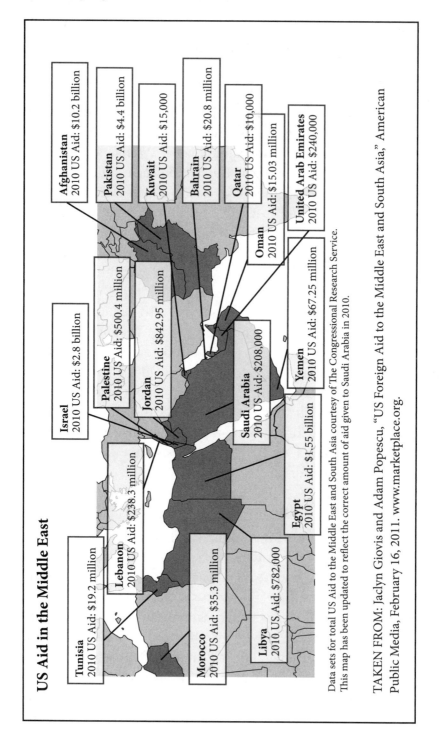

US Aid in the Middle East

Afghanistan
2010 US Aid: $10.2 billion

Pakistan
2010 US Aid: $4.4 billion

Kuwait
2010 US Aid: $15,000

Bahrain
2010 US Aid: $20.8 million

Qatar
2010 US Aid: $10,000

United Arab Emirates
2010 US Aid: $240,000

Oman
2010 US Aid: $15.03 million

Israel
2010 US Aid: $2.8 billion

Palestine
2010 US Aid: $500.4 million

Jordan
2010 US Aid: $842.95 million

Saudi Arabia
2010 US Aid: $208,000

Yemen
2010 US Aid: $67.25 million

Egypt
2010 US Aid: $1.55 billion

Tunisia
2010 US Aid: $19.2 million

Lebanon
2010 US Aid: $238.3 million

Morocco
2010 US Aid: $35.3 million

Libya
2010 US Aid: $782,000

Data sets for total US Aid to the Middle East and South Asia courtesy of The Congressional Research Service.
This map has been updated to reflect the correct amount of aid given to Saudi Arabia in 2010.

TAKEN FROM: Jaclyn Giovis and Adam Popescu, "US Foreign Aid to the Middle East and South Asia," American
Public Media, February 16, 2011. www.marketplace.org.

the prime minister would emerge from the victorious political party, not from backroom conversations in the royal palace. Electoral reforms are also promised, to end the gerrymandering that minimizes representation for Palestinian-origin Jordanians and creates a permanent majority for the East Bank tribes.

But those tribes have long been the Hashemites' [an Arab dynastic tribe] power base, and they man the army and the police, so such a reform is fraught with danger for the king. Past announcements of reform have never panned out, and high officials say the identity issue—Are the Palestinians "real" Jordanians, loyal to the Hashemite kingdom, or would they choose allegiance to a Palestinian state?—cannot be solved until a Palestinian state actually exists and offers them citizenship. So the pace of change to come in Jordan remains unclear, even if advisers to the king are insistent that his reading of the regional revolts has persuaded him he must move soon.

Morocco

The king of Morocco has announced an even deeper reform, one that would move the country to a true constitutional monarchy. He has called for separation of powers, independent courts, prime ministers who actually govern, and a reduction in the now central role of the palace. Morocco was already far from an absolute monarchy, but if this plan is implemented, it will provide a model for the Arab world— which is why there are stories in Arab circles that the Saudis have privately expressed extreme displeasure to the Moroccan king over the terrible precedent he is setting.

Other Gulf Countries

While Qatar and the United Arab Emirates can buy off their tiny citizenries, since their populations are made up mostly of guest workers who do not expect political rights, Saudi Arabia has a population of 25 million, many of whom are unemployed and unemployable young men, trained in the miserable Saudi school system only to recite the Koran and unfit for any work in a modern economy. The endless billions in oil wealth have produced inequality and excess; they have not produced development.

This month [March 2011], the king, aware of the dangers in this Arab Spring, announced a staggering $93 billion in subsidies—bribes, really—to head off trouble. Nothing he announced, however—better government salaries and pensions, for example, and the construction of 500,000 houses—will make the kingdom more productive or give ordinary Saudis real political rights. Local elections have been announced, but women will still not be permitted to vote, and elected officials will "share" power with royal appointees. The king also announced an expansion of his security forces by 60,000 and a larger budget for the religious police. This is not a reform program but a program designed to defeat reform.

Which monarchies will bend and not break, getting and staying ahead of the curve? Which will fall back when reform produces opposition, to be swept away by the region's new revolution of rising expectations? It is impossible to be certain, because in each case one man's vision and courage will determine the answer. Reformist kings can save their dynasties now by helping their countries move smoothly into democracy, or they will end their years in exile like the Russian aristocrats of a century earlier.

I *"Some parts of the U.S. government are better prepared for crises than others."*

The United States Should Better Prepare for Political Upheaval in the Middle East

Paul B. Stares

Paul B. Stares is a senior fellow for conflict prevention and director of the Center for Preventive Action at the Council on Foreign Relations. In the following viewpoint, he argues that the President Barack Obama administration was unprepared for the Arab Spring because of the failure of the US intelligence system to predict and address the growing unrest. Stares suggests that the United States should improve its early warning system by instituting a regular national security risk assessment of potential threats and challenges. In that way, he asserts, intelligence agencies can develop an overall strategy to avert or better address emerging crises like the Arab Spring.

As you read, consider the following questions:

1. What factors does Stares identify as impediments to an early warning system?

Paul B. Stares, "Enhancing U.S. Crisis Preparedness," Policy Innovation Memorandum no. 5, Council on Foreign Relations, June 2011. Copyright © 2011 by the Council on Foreign Relations. All rights reserved. Reproduced by permission.

2. Why does the author say that a 2005 presidential directive to improve strategic planning failed?

3. Why does the author think that the Obama administration should revive the National Security Policy Planning Committee (NSPPC)?

The [President Barack] Obama administration was caught flat-footed by the recent Arab Spring uprisings in the Middle East and North Africa. Not only did the intelligence community fail to warn senior officials of the combustible situations in Tunisia and Egypt, but evidently little or no forethought was given to how the United States might respond to popular uprisings or other forms of political instability in those countries of clear importance to U.S. interests and regional goals. As a result, the administration struggled to manage the unfolding crisis, largely improvising its responses without a clear sense of their implications or the overarching strategic objectives. The Obama administration can reduce its chances of being blindsided and unprepared in future crises by instituting a regular national security risk assessment of potential threats and challenges while also elevating the role of strategic planning to provide high-level policy guidance as to how they may be managed and, better still, averted. The capacity of the National Security Council and the State Department to handle complex contingencies should also be upgraded.

The Challenges

Crisis preparedness can be considered a function of three factors—early warning, pre-planning, and the availability of ready and adaptable resources. Each has its own set of challenges.

Early Warning

As numerous cases of strategic surprise have demonstrated, early warning can be impeded by a failure to identify critical signals amid background noise, counter various analytical biases that can distort the interpretation of incoming information, and minimize the bureaucratic barriers to the timely alerting of senior decision makers. The United States has invested heavily in intelligence gathering and analytical capabilities to address these challenges, but the sheer complexity and randomness of the many factors and interactions that can precipitate a major crisis make accurate and timely warning immensely difficult. It is hard to imagine how any early-warning system could have predicted the chain of events triggered by the self-immolation of a lowly fruit vendor in Tunisia in December 2010.

The difficulty of looking far into the future reinforces the tendency for senior policy makers to demand short-term "current intelligence" to help them manage events that could occur next week rather than next year. The need to warn of potentially catastrophic terrorist attacks and support current military operations in Iraq and Afghanistan has further accentuated this short-term focus. Thus, other than the annual unclassified global threat briefing by the director of national intelligence (DNI) to Congress, there is no regular and systematic process of "scanning the horizon" for either potentially threatening developments and contingencies or political opportunities that could arise.

Pre-Planning

Busy policy makers are understandably reluctant to expend precious time on planning for potential crises that may never materialize, especially those that seem particularly remote or seemingly inconsequential. With every crisis, there is also a natural resistance to make plans that may be irrelevant to the specific circumstances or quickly rendered meaningless. Policy makers also like to retain maximum freedom of maneuver in a crisis, which pre-planning threatens to restrict. As a result, while the Defense Department and combatant commands conduct extensive operational planning for specific military contingencies, very little strategic planning takes place within the U.S. government. The small policy planning bureau at the State Department is primarily used to support special initiatives or the day-to-day needs of the secretary, while the even smaller strategic planning directorate at the National Security Council (NSC) does more or less the same for the national security adviser.

Recent efforts to improve the level of strategic planning in the U.S. government have not fared well. A 2005 presidential directive authorizing the State Department "to coordinate interagency processes to identify states at risk of instability, lead interagency planning to prevent or mitigate conflict and develop detailed contingency plans for integrated United States government reconstruction and stabilization efforts" largely failed because the new coordinator for reconstruction and stabilization (S/CRS) tasked with this responsibility was never given the necessary resources or bureaucratic backing. Similarly, an NSC-led interagency group formed in the late stages of the George W. Bush administration to consider potential strategic challenges—the National Security Policy Planning Committee (NSPPC)—never gained traction within the mainstream policy process, and its work was largely ignored. The Obama administration chose not to reconstitute it or replace it with a similar interagency planning mechanism.

Ready and Adaptable Resources

Because crises are considered rare events, maintaining dedicated personnel and resources on standby to help manage them is generally deemed excessive. Preparing senior policy makers for specific contingencies through simulations and exercises is also exceedingly hard given the press of daily events. And Congress has traditionally resisted appropriating funds for unspecified emergencies. As a consequence, crises are typically managed in a makeshift manner: personnel are pulled from their regular assignments, responses are hastily prepared, and funds are hurriedly reprogrammed if they can be. Once the crisis is over, whatever the lessons or valuable experience gained in the process usually dissipates as life returns to "normal."

Some parts of the U.S. government are better prepared for crises than others. The Defense Department has considerable military and civilian resources at the ready as well as flexible contingency funding to draw on at short notice. Even the U.S. Agency for International Development (USAID) has a modest capability to respond to humanitarian and other emergencies. The State Department, however, continues to be hobbled by a limited crisis "surge capacity" and insufficient emergency funds. At the White House, the newly modernized Situation Room, with its state-of-the-art video conference facilities, has significantly enhanced high-level crisis management and coordination, but the NSC remains chronically understaffed. Valuable experience and operationally relevant guidance for future crises is not retained due to the regular turnover of personnel, especially between administrations.

Improving U.S. Crisis Anticipation, Planning, and Management

U.S. crisis preparedness can be enhanced by implementing these three recommendations:

1. Conduct a comprehensive U.S. national security risk assessment every two years at the behest of the national security adviser. This would evaluate potential threats and other plausible strategic challenges over a twelve-to-eighteen-month time frame using agreed-upon criteria for assessing their relative likelihood and impact. A useful model is the UK [United Kingdom] government's National Security Risk Assessment. This effort would be overseen by a newly created and properly staffed deputy national security adviser for strategic planning and carried out in partnership with the Office of the DNI. The Strategic Futures Group at the National Intelligence

Council, which has recently been formed from the disbanded National Warning Office, should be tasked to support this effort. Using the techniques of strategic foresight analysis, plausible scenarios of consequence to U.S. interests would be assessed on the basis of identifiable risk factors (e.g., autocratic regimes, demographic imbalances, prior history of conflict) as well as known crisis triggers (e.g., coups, a rigged election, food price spikes) and drivers (e.g., opportunities for public mobilization, regime fracturing, external intervention). The goal would be to not only anticipate potential risks but also envisage possible strategic opportunities.

2. Revive and elevate the status of the currently moribund NSPPC for the purpose of directing and coordinating interagency policy planning. The new deputy national security adviser for strategic planning would chair the committee, which would meet at the assistant secretary level. A list of planning priorities based on the findings of the national security risk assessment would be generated and approved by the principals committee of the NSC. The principal planning departments of the relevant bureaus would conduct the bulk of the planning under the direction of the deputy national security adviser. The intent would not be to develop detailed operational plans but rather identify broad policy options to lessen the likelihood of a specific threat or undesired crisis from materializing and mitigate the potential negative consequences if it did. These planning documents would be reviewed twice a year by the deputies committee of the NSC, which would recommend revisions and direct follow-on action.

3. Establish a separate directorate for complex contingency operations within the NSC to oversee and coordinate humanitarian relief and crisis stabilization missions

across the U.S. government. Its directing staff should preferably not be short-term political appointees. Reforms identified in the 2010 Quadrennial Diplomacy and Development Review to enhance in-house capacity for crisis prevention and response at the State Department and USAID need to be implemented and fully funded by Congress. These include the development of an interagency international operational response framework to facilitate government coordination, a roster of on-call experts with proven functional and regional expertise that can be assembled and even deployed at short notice, and a complex crises fund for unforeseen contingencies.

Periodical and Internet Sources Bibliography

The following articles have been selected to supplement the diverse views presented in this chapter.

Anne Applebaum	"Not So Fast," *Slate*, March 7, 2011.
Doug Bandow	"Libya: Another Unnecessary War of Choice," *Forbes*, March 14, 2011.
Bob Confer	"The Moral Propaganda for U.S. Intervention in Libya," *New American*, May 7, 2011.
Michael Gerson	"Obama Is Dragged into Doing the Right Thing on Libya," *Washington Post*, March 21, 2011.
Charles Krauthammer	"From Baghdad to Benghazi," *Washington Post*, March 4, 2011.
Alan J. Kuperman	"False Pretense for War In Libya?," *Boston Globe*, April 14, 2011.
Andrew C. McCarthy	"No Intervention in Libya," *National Review Online*, March 10, 2011. www.nationalreview.com.
Romesh Ratnesar	"Libya: The Case for U.S. Intervention," *Time*, March 7, 2011.
Michael Rubin	"The Road to Tahrir Square," *Commentary*, March 2011.
Robert Satloff	"Obama's Delicate Middle East Pivot," Real Clear World, May 19, 2011. www.realclearworld.com.
Jonathan S. Tobin	"Bad Day for Libya Intervention Critics," *Commentary*, August 22, 2011.

CHAPTER 4

What Are the Social and Political Effects of the Arab Spring?

Chapter Preface

To mark the anniversary of the September 11, 2001, terrorist attacks on the United States, the acknowledged leader of al Qaeda since the death of Osama bin Laden in May 2011, Ayman al-Zawahiri, released a video with a special message: al Qaeda supports the Arab Spring and hopes that it will usher in an era of strict Islamic law in the Arab world. Zawahiri went on to say that the Arab Spring should be considered a defeat for the United States and a victory for fundamentalist groups such as al Qaeda. He concluded, "The blessed rebellious Arab earthquake has turned America's calculations over heels."

The trouble with Zawahiri's triumphant statement is that many in the Arab world and the West disagree with him. In fact, most analysts agree that the Arab Spring shows that militant jihadism has failed. Instead of turning to al Qaeda, the people rose and made change happen themselves. The people protesting for change were demanding political and economic justice and democratic reform, not for support of Islamic fundamentalism or al Qaeda. Corrupt leaders like Hosni Mubarak in Egypt and Muammar Gaddafi in Libya were overthrown without the aid of terrorist groups; they were ousted by the efforts of grassroots movements of regular people looking for a chance at political and economic self-determination.

For many analysts, al Qaeda's declining role in the Arab world began almost immediately after September 11, 2001, the day the successful terrorist attacks masterminded by the terrorist group on targets in New York City and Washington, DC, took place. Leading Islamic groups once tolerant or even sympathetic to the aims of al Qaeda were appalled at the attacks and began to distance themselves. In Iraq and Afghanistan, al Qaeda often targeted other Muslims and caused hardships for communities hoping for peace. A number of jihadists and Islamic figures were openly critical about al Qaeda's tactics and began to explore nonviolent ways to achieve their goals: overthrowing dictatorial and corrupt regimes and a greater sense of self-determination.

One example of this shift in approach is Al-Gama'a al-Islamiyya (the Islamic Group), a former al Qaeda ally that cooperated in the assassination of Egyptian president Anwar el-Sadat in 1981 and was implicated in the 1993 World Trade Center bombing in New York. The Islamic Group has rejected political violence and terrorism and works to change the political system through conventional means, including founding a political party and sponsoring candidates in democratic elections.

Another example is Zawahiri's old terrorist group, the Egyptian Islamic Jihad. Several of its factions continue to support terrorist tactics, but many others eschew its efforts and are highly critical of al Qaeda. These nonviolent factions are working to form a political party in Egypt and to participate in upcoming political elections.

Experts hail this as a welcome trend: groups that once embraced terrorist tactics and allied themselves with al Qaeda are now turning to nonviolent and more productive means of affecting the political process. As onetime allies turn away from al Qaeda and the War on Terror eliminates top leaders like Osama bin Laden, Anwar al-Awlaki, and Abu Hafs al-Shahri, many analysts believe that the terrorist group is becoming more isolated and has perhaps worn out its welcome in the Arab world.

Yet as Zawahiri's message about the Arab Spring shows, al Qaeda still has some tricks up its sleeve. By taking credit for the conditions that caused the Arab Spring and deeming it a decisive defeat for the United States, al Qaeda continues to position itself as champion of the Arab world and a persistent and dangerous threat to the United States.

The impact of the Arab Spring on al Qaeda is one of the subjects discussed in the following chapter, which examines the political and social impact of the Arab Spring. Other viewpoints included in the chapter explore the movement's effect on women, gays, and religious minorities.

> "It is easier to oust a regime than it is to help put something clearly better in its place."

The Arab Spring Has Destabilized the Middle East

Richard N. Haass

Richard N. Haass is the president of the Council on Foreign Relations. In the following viewpoint, he expresses his concern that the Arab Spring has destabilized the political dynamics of the region. He fears that Arab leaders, under pressure from reformers and protesters, will decide to fight and embark on campaigns of brutal violence and repression instead of considering even minor reforms. He also worries that less tolerant and stable governments will emerge and that terrorist groups will gain more traction in certain areas. Haass suggests that the United States should continue to provide assistance as long as reforms are implemented and military intervention is avoided.

As you read, consider the following questions:

1. How many people does the author say have been killed in recent fighting in the Arab world?

2. According to the author, what are the most organized groups in Arab societies?

3. How does Haass characterize the relationship between Israelis and Palestinians?

Tunisia, Egypt, Bahrain, Yemen, and Libya have had their turn; now Syria occupies centre stage. More than 1,000 people have been killed in recent fighting, while hundreds of thousands still risk their lives challenging the regime. Syria's future rests on whether a handful of Alawite [a branch of Shia Islam] generals are prepared to keep killing their fellow citizens to preserve the [President Bashar al-]Assad regime and, more fundamentally, Alawite primacy. The outside world, fearing the alternative and bogged down in Libya, is little more than a bystander. Syria's violence is just one further sign that the promise of the Arab Spring has given way to a long, hot summer in which the geopolitics of the Middle East are being reset for the worse.

The Stalling of the Arab Spring

Syria is not unique. Other threatened leaders around the regions have clearly now decided against emulating the former presidents of Tunisia and Egypt, who went gently into the night. Violence, along with the threat of imprisonment and international tribunals, has persuaded them that the future is winner takes all and loser loses all. Not surprisingly, they have chosen to resist.

Meanwhile, the most organised groups in Arab societies tend to be the army and other security organs on one hand and Islamist entities on the other. Secular liberal groups (if they exist) tend to be weak and divided, and unlikely to prevail in any political competition in the near term. Facebook and Twitter matter but not enough.

Looked at more broadly, the stalling of the Arab Spring has both revealed and widened the breach between the US and Saudi Arabia. Saudi leaders were alienated by what they saw as the US abandoning the regime in Egypt after three decades of close cooperation. The Americans, for their part, were unhappy with the Saudi decision to intervene militarily in Bahrain. But such independent, uncoordinated policies are now likely to become more frequent, especially if international efforts to stop Iran's nuclear program come up short.

The Effects of the Arab Spring

Iran itself has both gained and lost from recent events. Higher oil prices, the fall of the staunchly anti-Iranian regime in Egypt, and projected reductions in US military presence in Iraq and Afghanistan have all strengthened its hand. These gains are offset at least in part by the weakened status of Iran's close partner Syria—and by signs that Iran's leadership is divided against itself.

The effects go wider still. Relations between Israelis and Palestinians are increasingly strained. Israelis are more reluctant than ever to make concessions in light of the disarray on their borders, while the new voice for Arab publics emerging from the upheavals makes it more difficult for Arab governments to compromise. And while terrorist groups had nothing to do with the upheavals, they are in a position to benefit as governments with strong antiterrorist records are weakened or ousted. Signs of exactly this are popping up in Yemen, and it is only a matter of time before they do so in Libya.

Take all this together, and you see a series of developments that are beginning to produce a region that is less tolerant, less prosperous, and less stable than what existed. To be sure, the authoritarian old guard that still dominates much of the Middle East could yet be forced or eased out and replaced with something relatively democratic and open. Unfortunately, the odds now seem against this happening.

Ed Stein. Reprinted with permission.

A US Plan

What, then, can outsiders do to affect the course of events? The honest answer is not all that much. Interests are greater than influence. There is little in foreign policy more difficult than trying to steer the course of reform in another country.

That doesn't mean that there is nothing to be done. Wherever possible, wise outsiders should promote gradual political change. Constitutions need to be rewritten, checks and balances created. But economics counts as much as politics, if not more. This means providing assistance, so long as reforms are implemented. The scale of the generosity should be matched by the scale of the conditionality.

Elsewhere, it is still worth exploring further the role diplomacy can play in reducing tensions between Israelis and Palestinians. But the Quartet [referring to the United Nations, the United States, the European Union, and Russia] needs to work with, not dictate to, local parties. Launching a new negotiation is surely preferable to taking the issue to the UN General Assembly, where positions are likely to harden. In addition, the process of building a modern, effective Palestinian state from the ground up in the West Bank needs to be accelerated.

Simple Lessons

Yet the most important lessons from the Arab Spring are also the simplest. Military intervention should, as a rule, be avoided. It is easier to oust a regime than it is to help put something clearly better in its place. Iraq, Afghanistan, and Libya all stand as warnings. Islamists who eschew violence should be talked to, not written off. And no one should be lulled by recent drops in oil prices: The world is only one major crisis in Saudi Arabia away from $200 per barrel oil. Governments might want to use the respite to take additional steps to reduce their dependence on the region's energy resources. There is no better hedge against the strong possibility that it will not be springtime any time soon in the Middle East.

> "*Provided Islamists say they accept the rules of the peaceful democratic game, as the mainstream ones now do, they must be given their chance to take up the reins of power, if that is what people say they want at the ballot box.*"

The Arab Spring Provides an Opportunity for Islamists and Secularists to Forge Peace

The Economist

The Economist *is a weekly news and international affairs publication. In the following viewpoint, the author views the Arab Spring as an opportunity to bring Islamist groups into the democratic process and to forge working, inclusive governments. For years, the author asserts, Arab governments have tried to repress Islamist movements, and it hasn't worked. It is time, according to the author, that the secular and religious forces work together to find some accommodation to shape the future of the Middle East and North Africa.*

As you read, consider the following questions:

1. According to the author, what have the strongmen of North Africa and the Middle East been telling their Western supporters about an Islamist takeover?

2. What are Salafists, according to the author?

3. How many years of stagnation does the author say have been affecting the Arab world?

For years the strongmen of North Africa and the Middle East told their Western supporters that they were all that stood between the Arab world and an Islamist takeover. In fact Islam did not inspire the Arab Spring—not even in Egypt, where the Muslim Brotherhood had long been the main opposition to the autocracy of Hosni Mubarak. But were the autocrats right all along? In the wake of revolution, Islamist movements have been gaining ground. Political parties under the banner of Islam may well emerge after genuine elections later this year [2011] as the biggest in rejuvenated Tunisian and Egyptian parliaments. This makes many secular liberals across the Arab world nervous lest the Islamists hijack the revolutions, turning them into vehicles for repressive and intolerant regimes.

Such fears are understandable, but they should not get in the way of democracy. Provided Islamists say they accept the rules of the peaceful democratic game, as the mainstream ones now do, they must be given their chance to take up the reins of power, if that is what people say they want at the ballot box. The Arab world has tried suppression (and the West shamefully connived in it), and it did not work.

Facing the Threat

To give Islamists their head is indeed a risk. In the past few days Salafists, who preach a version of Islam that harks back to the puritanical zealotry of the early days, have assaulted lib-

The Strength of the Muslim Brotherhood

Because the Muslim Brotherhood is still a secretive, cell-based organization, and because it operates mostly underground, there are no reliable estimates either of its strength or its potential electoral base. Analysts have placed its membership as low as 100,000 nationwide and as high as a million or more. Similarly, some experts say that in a free and fair election the Brothers would win as little as 10 percent of the vote or as much as 20 to 40 percent—and their share will probably be higher the sooner the election is held, since they are by far the best organized force at the moment.

Robert Dreyfuss, *"What Is the Muslim Brotherhood, and Will It Take Over Egypt,"* Mother Jones, *February 11, 2011.*

eral protesters in Tahrir Square [in Cairo, Egypt]. Last month in Tunis [the capital of Tunisia] Salafists smashed a cinema that was showing a mildly provocative film falsely said to defame Islam. Some secular democrats fear that if the tyrants hanging on in Libya and Syria are toppled they will be replaced by the nastier type of Islamist.

But these fears should not be overblown. The term Islamist covers a wide spectrum. The Salafists are a small minority. The new Islamist mainstream, which includes Egypt's Muslim Brotherhood and Tunisia's [Ennahda] party, has evolved over the years, and now realises that the dominant new generation of young Arabs using Facebook and YouTube will never kowtow to the anachronistic sort of imam who once seemed to hold sway in the Islamist camp. Mainstream Islamists, the modernising majority, now insist that they would uphold women's rights, that they would not force women to wear the veil, that they would not ban alcohol, that they would respect ethnic and religious minorities (especially Egypt's millions of edgy Copts [a Christian religious group]) and that they would not universally impose *sharia* law. These more pragmatic sorts argue that they deserve the chance to prove that they are sincere in espousing pluralistic politics. Encouraging secular parties to gang up against them or having them banned altogether, as courts in Turkey once used to do in order to defend the secular order, is more likely to push Islamists underground, to unite factions that would otherwise work against each other and even to foment violence.

Many sceptical secular Arabs will say that they have heard such assurances before. The Islamists are fooling you. They are playing a long game. They are bound to sound ever-so-moderate to begin with, to ensure that the still powerful military establishments in such places as Egypt give them their head, as now seems likely. The Islamists with their honeyed words still intend, say the doubters, to undertake a long march through the institutions of state, as Communists once tried to do in Europe. After winning a slice of power, even if they at first agree to share a coalition government, they will gradually accrue all of it, establishing the Iranian-style supremacy of Islam in government. And, if people turn against them at the polls, they will never let go.

Only One Path to Tread

The behaviour of Turkey's Islamists, to whom the Arab ones now look for inspiration, suggests this is too pessimistic. Despite worrying recent signs of authoritarianism, the Turks have in general shown religious moderation and constitutional rectitude, and have successfully tamed a coup-prone army. Their democratic credentials will be proven only when they give up power after an election defeat, but after nine years in office they seem wedded to the ballot box, bolstering the notion that Islam and democracy can coexist. In Egypt and Tu-

nisia the best protection against a creeping Islamist takeover—
and an early test—will be new constitutions that separate
mosque and state and enshrine minority rights.

People will continue to wrangle over relations between the
state and religion in the Arab world, just as they did for cen-
turies in Europe. But after 30 years of stagnation it is clear
that neither religious sentiment nor popular political aspirations can be suppressed. These two great forces, Islam and democracy, must find some accommodation; and how they do
so will shape the future of the Middle East.

"The Christian community's hope of equality in freedom of speech and freedom of worship within pluralist democracies is being brutally obstructed by the Islamic extremists. Yet it is too early to despair."

The Arab Spring Has Ushered in Religious Intolerance and Persecution

Jonathan Aitken

Jonathan Aitken is an author and columnist for the American Spectator. *In the following viewpoint, he maintains that the Arab Spring has allowed a wave of intolerance, discrimination, and violence to wash over the region's religious minorities, particularly the Christian population in countries such as Egypt and Iraq. Aitken reports that Islamist political parties have gained power and have implemented brutal campaigns of repression and intimidation against Christian populations. He fears the future looks grim for Christians in the Middle East and North Africa.*

As you read, consider the following questions:

1. How many Coptic Christians does the author say live in Egypt?

2. According to the author, how many Christians were killed on New Year's Day 2011?

3. What percentage of Iraqi Christians have migrated, according to the author?

The Arab Spring is fast becoming a winter of discontent for Christians and other religious minorities in the Middle East. In Washington the first stirrings of protest were hailed as a breakthrough for democracy. But the second phase of the uprising has brought fear, discrimination, and violent pressure against Christians in countries rebelling against incumbent regimes across the region.

This is particularly disappointing because the early signs of tolerance were hopeful. One of the most moving aspects of the crowds in Tahrir Square [in Egypt] was that Christians and Muslims protested alongside each other in unity. Such was their solidarity that at prayer time on Friday [in June 2011] the Christians formed a human shield to protect their kneeling fellow demonstrators from police baton charges. The cooperation was reciprocated but it was too good to last.

The Case of the Coptic Christians

Egypt's 8 million Coptic Christians [Egypt Christianity] are now having a rough time. The vacuum left by [ousted Egyptian president Hosni] Mubarak is being filled by the Muslim Brotherhood [an Islamist political party] and the Salafists [a sect of Islam]. Both are extreme in their Islamism. They campaigned for their followers to vote "yes" to the new and flawed constitutional proposals that will result in discrimination against religious minorities, women, secular organizations, and progressive youth groups. Small wonder that when the "yes" vote was confirmed to have won, the ultraconservative Salafist leader Sheikh Muhammad Hussein Yacoub was quoted as saying, "That's it. The country is ours."

There are sinister signs of the anti-Christian direction in which the Islamic extremists want to take Egypt. On New Year's Day, 21 Christians were killed and another 70 injured by a bomb that exploded as worshippers were leaving midnight mass at al-Qidissin (The Saints) church in Alexandria. On March 8, 13 Christians died and another 70 were injured when Salafists attacked Copts who were demonstrating against the tearing down of their church in Sool village and the murder of a priest in Assiut. On March 20, Salafists in the town of Qena cut off the ears of 45-year-old Coptic Christian Ayman Anwar Mitri after accusing him of having had an affair with a Muslim woman. These episodes are part of a continuing pattern of outrages, including lynchings and beatings of Copts. In a lecture given in London on April 8 [2011], the Anglican leader in Egypt, Bishop Mouneer Hanna Anis, said, "The plight of the Coptic Christians is getting worse. They are living in a climate of uncertainty, fear, and apprehension."

A Menacing New World

Bishop Mouneer's words apply to minority religious communities all across the region that some Washington commentators have far too optimistically hailed as "the new Middle East." If the Salafists, jihadists, and Muslim Brothers have their way it will become the medieval Middle East, notorious for its intolerance and persecution of Christians. Who is going to prevent this?

Until recently it was a strange paradox that some of the most repressive political regimes were protective of religious minorities. In Syria, the beleaguered Bashar al-Assad has a good record of safeguarding the rights of the Druze, the Christians, and the Jews. As a traveler to Damascus in 2008, I was moved by visiting the well-preserved Christian churches and

What America Can Do

While Washington cannot impose tolerance on the new Egypt, American officials can point to the danger posed by virulent Islamists to that nation's future. If the radicals grow in influence, they are likely to sweep away more than the vulnerable Coptic population. They might take down the new political system, with dangerous consequences for Egypt and beyond.

Doug Bandow, *"What Kind of Revolution?,"*
American Spectator, *July 13, 2011.*

holy places of the city, including those on Straight Street. They are not much changed since the blinded Saul of Tarsus had his sight restored there by Ananias and was lowered down the wall in a basket to escape his pursuers. I also saw the tomb of John the Baptist that President Assad visits once a year to lead a Christian prayer ceremony. Such tolerance is unlikely to last. The regime, even if it survives, will have to dilute its secularism by further concessions to its Islamist partners like Iran, Hezbollah, and Hamas.

If you want to understand how grim the future looks for Christians in the Middle East, go to Baghdad, where the continuing sectarian violence has driven most of them out of the city and the country. Once they worshipped peacefully under Saddam Hussein. Now, 80 percent of Iraqi Christians have emigrated. Those that remain are mainly elderly, although there are heroic younger congregations who literally have to fight the good fight to remain churchgoers.

Canon Andrew White

One of the bravest men I know is Canon Andrew White, vicar of St. George's, Baghdad and author of *Faith Under Fire*

(Monarch Books, 2011). I recently shared a platform with him at a Christian Solidarity Worldwide event in London. As we discussed the situation in the Arab world, I was moved to tears by his description of what he and his flock have to endure.

"Christianity in Iraq is under very vicious attack," says White. "It is a question of abduction, bombing, torture, rape, and murder. Christians are forced to pay *jizya*, the tax historically imposed by Islamic states on non-Muslims—in effect, protection money. So things are very difficult. Last year alone 93 members of my congregations were killed. The threat is particularly great for those who convert to Christianity. I baptized 13 adults secretly last year. Eleven of them were dead within a week."

Occasionally the deaths of persecuted Christians send shock waves in the right direction. One of the first casualties of the Tunisian revolution was a Polish priest, murdered for his faith by jihadists. His martyrdom caused protests in the streets that produced clear statements in favor of religious diversity by the new regime. Would that this example might prevail in other countries. Unfortunately all the signs point to greater intolerance.

Growing Intolerance and Discrimination

Away from the dramatic episodes of bombings, assassinations, and ear or limb amputations by Islamist extremists, the everyday reality of life for Christians in the Middle East is that they face increasingly uncomfortable experiences of discrimination. Thanks to subtle or often unsubtle Islamist pressures, Christians have far less chance of employment in such organizations as the police, the military, the universities, the teaching professions, and the government bureaucracy. They also find themselves at a disadvantage in matters like housing or the issuing of driving licenses. One of their many problems is that they are suspected of being pro-Western. This is odd since more than 70 percent of Middle East Christians are from the Oriental Orthodox Churches—Armenian, Syrian, and Coptic—while an Eastern Catholic Church with the Maronites and the Chaldeans forms the second largest group in the region. The doctrinal differences between these elements go back to the historic ecumenical Councils of Nicaea, Constantinople, and Ephesus, held respectively in AD 325, 381, and 431. It has taken the Arab Spring of 2011 to put them on the front line of hostility and persecution.

When the popular demonstrations against unpopular Arab rulers began earlier this year, the Christian churches in the region saw the movement with mixed emotions of hope and fear. Sadly, fear is now in the ascendant. The Christian community's hope of equality in freedom of speech and freedom of worship within pluralist democracies is being brutally obstructed by the Islamic extremists. Yet it is too early to despair. These revolutions have some way to go and many of their younger and more moderate Muslim supporters know that intolerant Islamism is not the answer to the problem of how to change society for the better. We Westerners should watch and pray!

> "This year's changes in the Middle East
> and North Africa have had a profound
> impact on the prospects for peace in
> the region."

The Arab Spring Complicates
the Palestinian Peace Process

Salman Shaikh

*Salman Shaikh is director of the Brookings Doha Center and a
fellow at the Saban Center for Middle East Policy at the Brookings Institution. In the following viewpoint, he contends that the
Palestinians found solidarity with the Arab Spring goals of
greater self-determination and justice that has worked to complicate their situation with the Israelis. Shaikh reports that Palestinians are more aggressive in their demands for statehood and
are organizing large protests that have many Israelis worried. He
argues that a serious international effort is needed to broker a
peace deal between the two countries.*

As you read, consider the following questions:

1. How many Palestinians does the author say are on Facebook in the West Bank and Gaza alone?

2. According to the author, what did President Obama
   mention as a basis for peace talks between Israel and
   Palestine that provoked a sharp response from Israeli
   prime minister Benjamin Netanyahu?

3. What does the author say the situation between Israel
   and Palestine requires?

It is often said by people in the Middle East, especially Israelis and Palestinians, that "in the end, we always come back
to the Arab-Israeli conflict." That is exactly what happened on
Thursday, May 19 [2011], when U.S. President Barack Obama
delivered a major policy speech at the State Department, in-
troducing new principles for negotiations based on 1967 borders, and this past weekend, when at least 10 unarmed protesters were killed by Israeli fire on a day the Palestinians call
the "Nakba," or "Catastrophe." The Arab-Israeli conflict is
once again front and center.

But if the broad brush strokes of this story are by now
painfully familiar, the context and the particulars of this week
may point to a different kind of flare-up while the United
States seeks to restart peace talks. There is, of course, the Arab
Spring: The Palestinians see the new narrative of the Arab revolts for greater freedoms, justice, and equality joining their
own decades-old search for the same, and for a state of their
own. For Israelis, Sunday, May 15, was the day when the Arab
awakening washed up on their own still provisional borders,
reminding them yet again of how vulnerable they are and
how isolated they have become.

Coordinated protests on Israel's 1949 armistice lines with
Syria and Lebanon—as well as in the West Bank, Gaza, Egypt,
and Jordan—have alarmed many Israelis and raised concerns
that Israel lacks the practical means to counter mass demonstrations in the future. In fact, only a heavy security presence
near the Egyptian and Jordanian borders with Israel prevented
protesters from besieging these areas as well. Israelis are realiz-

ing the tangible effects of a rapidly changing region in which old certainties are dying and fears of a return to conflict are revived.

The Arab Spring Comes to Palestine

Palestinian refugees, meanwhile, used the tools of today's revolutions—the Internet in general and Facebook in particular—to organize protests and assert their right to return to their homes in what is now Israel. An estimated 600,000 Palestinians are on Facebook in the West Bank and Gaza alone, and nearly one-third of them are thought to be politically influenced by social media. When Fatah [a Palestinian political party] and Hamas [a political party that governs the Gaza Strip] finally signed a reconciliation agreement two weeks ago in Cairo, they were responding in part to a campaign for Palestinian unity organized by Internet activists that had managed to mobilize thousands in both the West Bank and Gaza. Emboldened by these developments, activists are organizing more mass protests and marches to pressure Israel, the international community, and their own leadership as the Palestinian-imposed deadline for statehood approaches in September.

What made this year's Nakba Day all the more remarkable, though, were the events along the Syrian-Israeli de facto border. Thirty-eight years of near-total calm along the nearly 50-mile frontier were shattered as dozens of Palestinian protesters trampled their way through the security fence into the Israel-occupied Golan Heights. The event marked a failure for Israeli intelligence and the military and showed the impotence of the 1,250-member United Nations observer force established to monitor the 1974 Separation of Forces Agreement. It also showed that Bashar al-Assad's Baathist regime is ready to export instability if necessary, especially to Israel; given the degree of restrictions on movement in the area, it is inconceivable that the protesters could have reached the security fence without the acquiescence and participation of the Syrian authorities and security forces.

With the situation in Syria likely to worsen in the weeks ahead, was the breach a power play from a regime determined to reinforce the point that only it can ensure stability? Or was this a means of diverting attention from Syria's own crackdown and bolstering Assad's credentials as a resistance regime against Israel? In fact, it was likely both. The move may have backfired, however, leading Israel's military to conclude that Assad and his regime cannot be relied upon to deliver calm along their sensitive border. With May 15's events, the assertion that only with Assad comes stability and after him there is chaos has already been turned on its head. This is the moment for the international community to send a clear signal that it will not tolerate being blackmailed by the Assad regime, especially when the region's stability and security are at stake.

Renewing the Peace Talk Process

Obama's speech on Thursday proved that American and Israeli leaders can put off talking about these issues, but not for long. The president's mention of the 1967 borders as a basis for talks with the Palestinians provoked a sharp response from Prime Minister Benjamin Netanyahu even before he got on the plane to Washington, where he is due to meet with Obama May 20 and speak to a joint session of Congress on May 24. Netanyahu rejected Israel's withdrawal to such "indefensible" borders. As *Haaretz* columnist Aluf Benn opined in his recent editorial, Netanyahu's aim is to bolster Israel's defenses against the third intifada—not present major concessions.

By offering ideas on future security arrangements for a demilitarized Palestinian state as well as borders, Obama has finally laid out parameters on two of the four main issues (the others being Jerusalem and refugees) of the conflict. He also stressed the importance of a contiguous and viable Palestinian state that borders Egypt and Jordan, but rejected the idea that Palestinians could establish a state through a vote at the United Nations in September.

Is It Too Late?

The problem is that these ideas have come two years too late. The parties aren't speaking to one another, and their last attempt to do so only showed how far apart they are. There are also serious doubts as to whether the U.S. president has the political will and political strategy to push both Israelis and Palestinians as he campaigns for reelection. At best, Obama has pressed another reset button in order to start talks. He has not explained a clear way forward other than a vague call for the United States, the Middle East quartet [referring to the United Nations, United States, European Union, and Russia], and Arab states "to continue every effort to get beyond the current impasse." Meanwhile, Palestinian leaders, particularly President Mahmoud Abbas, feel freed by the Palestinian unity deal and will likely pursue their efforts for recognition of a Palestinian state at the United Nations if serious negotiations do not start soon—despite Obama's explicit rejection of this move.

This year's changes in the Middle East and North Africa have had a profound impact on the prospects for peace in the region. The people of the Arab world are no longer willing to play by the old rules, in which peacemaking is determined by Israel's security concerns and the United States' electoral calendar. There is a growing impatience to ensure justice for the Palestinians and a state of their own. Serious moves are required, therefore, to establish two states, Israel and Palestine, this year. The situation requires a new international effort similar to the Madrid conference that followed the first Gulf War in 1991. Back then, it was U.S. leadership that brought new impetus to achieve peace between Arabs and Israelis. This time, clear parameters on borders and security arrangements, as presented by Obama on Thursday, as well as the other core issues, could provide the basis and impetus for a final-status deal.

Failing that, the relevance of both Israeli concerns and American efforts will continue to recede as the Palestinians seize the initiative in an environment dictated by Arab popular will. It promises to be a long, hot summer in the Middle East.

> *"The political, economic, and cultural stagnation that al Qaeda fed off for more than two decades has been replaced by the fastest moving change the region has ever witnessed, the most promising of Arab Springs."*

The Arab Spring Makes al Qaeda Less Relevant

Paul Cruickshank

Paul Cruickshank is a CNN terrorism analyst. In the following viewpoint, he argues that the political and economic reform brought about by the Arab Spring has captured the imagination of Arab youth and has made al Qaeda a much less attractive and necessary option in the fight for justice and opportunity. Cruickshank notes that the fact that Egyptian protesters were able to oust President Hosni Mubarak without much bloodshed proves to many that al Qaeda is in decline and holds little promise for the people of the Middle East. However, he warns that al Qaeda may try to exploit various opportunities in some of the political instability in the region to grab power and advance its own goals.

As you read, consider the following questions:

1. What did al Qaeda leader Zawahiri write about the Mubarak regime in an April 2008 online chat with supporters, according to Cruickshank?

2. Why does the author think that Zawahiri's statement on Mubarak's ouster was so delayed?

3. What breakaway terrorist group do experts think is trying to relaunch itself after the fall of the Mubarak regime, according to the viewpoint?

When historians in future years grapple with the significance of the overthrow of the [Hosni] Mubarak regime in Egypt 10 days ago [February 11, 2011], coming as it did in the wake of the "Jasmine" January 14 revolution in Tunisia, they may judge it not only as a seismic event, shattering and renewing the Arab political order, but also the key watershed moment in confronting the global al Qaeda threat.

The political, economic, and cultural stagnation that al Qaeda fed off for more than two decades has been replaced by the fastest moving change the region has ever witnessed, the most promising of Arab Springs.

Eliminating the Need for al Qaeda

The burgeoning democracy movement across the Middle East appears to have caught al Qaeda off guard and threatens to reduce the terrorist group to irrelevance.

"If you have freedom, al Qaeda will go away," said Osama Rushdi, a former Egyptian jihadist.

"Al Qaeda can work under a dictatorship regime, but I think if we open the door for all people to be part of society and have human rights, then there will be security not just in Egypt but around the world," Rushdi told CNN.

The Danger Is Not Gone

But others caution that the coming years will not be without dangers.

In the case of Yemen, for example, some have suggested that protests may weaken the government's ability to confront al Qaeda's growing presence in the tribal areas of the country.

Furthermore, the weakening of security services throughout the Arab world may allow jihadist groups like al Qaeda in the medium term to rebuild capabilities, warns Noman Benotman, a former Libyan jihadist once personally acquainted with al Qaeda leaders, including Osama bin Laden and Ayman al-Zawahiri.

"This is a make or break moment for al Qaeda," said Benotman, now a senior analyst at the Quilliam Foundation, a UK [United Kingdom] counter-extremist think tank.

Al Qaeda's Attitude Toward the Arab Spring

In the short term, Benotman says, al Qaeda will need to navigate strong countervailing winds. The clamor by protesters from North Africa to the Gulf for more democracy is hardly change al Qaeda can believe in.

"What we see playing out now is completely against what al Qaeda is preaching," Benotman said.

In an April 2008 online Q&A with supporters, al Qaeda's no. 2 Zawahiri wrote that the only alternative to the Mubarak regime was setting up an Islamic state in Egypt, by which he meant an al Qaeda–style theocracy.

"Change (in Egypt) is coming—with Allah's permission—without a doubt, for this corrupt, rotten regime cannot possibly continue. The important thing is getting ready for change and being patient in that and preparing to accept sacrifices, then making use of the opportunities," he wrote.

A Less Attractive Option

But now, faced with a script they never expected, al Qaeda's top leadership could be in danger of losing the plot.

The televised scenes of secular, middle-class youngsters and Egyptians from all walks of life courageously, peacefully and ultimately successfully challenging the rule of President Hosni Mubarak have been transmitted onto tens of millions of television screens across the Arab world and have captured the imagination, providing vastly more attractive role models for young Arabs, whose hopes for too long have been strangled.

Delayed Response from al Qaeda's No. 2

From Zawahiri, who has regularly weighed in on political events in Egypt, there finally appeared to be a reaction—of sorts—to the Egyptian protests in a tape released on the Internet on Friday.

In the audio statement, al Qaeda's no. 2 neither directly acknowledges the protests nor the removal from power of Mubarak, instead referring to "what happened and happens in Egypt." The statement was dated the second Islamic lunar month of Safar, which corresponded to the period between January 6 and February 3, indicating that it was recorded at least a week before Mubarak left office. Demonstrations gathered pace in Egypt on January 25.

In his statement, Zawahiri as usual railed against the Mubarak regime but also criticized democracy as a system of government, hardly sentiment that endeared him to the millions thronging that day into Tahrir Square and other locations in Egypt to celebrate a "Day of Joy."

Self-preservation may explain Zawahiri's slow response.

According to data provided to CNN by IntelCenter, an American company that tracks al Qaeda statements, Zawahiri two years ago managed to get messages out as quickly as 10 days after a news event. But in the past year, his fastest response time was 32 days, suggesting that intensified U.S. drone strikes in the tribal areas of Pakistan may have pushed him into deeper hiding.

When he recorded the just-released message, it was possible that events could still play into his hands. During the first days of February the stakes in Egypt's Tahrir Square for al Qaeda and the United States could hardly have been higher.

The al Qaeda Narrative

As the protests gathered strength, it appeared possible that the Mubarak regime might move to crush the demonstrators and that Arab street protesters would view the United States as complicit.

Such a crackdown, and the frustration of raised expectations across the region, could have created a newly receptive climate for al Qaeda's key propaganda message—that the United States deliberately props up Middle Eastern dictatorships to prevent the emergence of an Islamic world power—and no doubt Zawahiri and other al Qaeda leaders would have exploited it to try to win recruits. But the ground shifted, Mubarak fell, and the United States strengthened its support for the demonstrators, hollowing out the al Qaeda narrative.

When in the coming weeks Zawahiri finally acknowledges Mubarak's exit, he will probably be seen by most Egyptians as more out of touch than ever. "He has no popularity in Egypt anymore," said Rushdi, the former Egyptian jihadist.

Rushdi spent time with Zawahiri in Peshawar in the late 1980s and remembers how Zawahiri and a number of other Egyptians with key leadership positions within al Qaeda influenced the world view of bin Laden and pushed his fledgling organization toward armed confrontation with Arab regimes.

Rushdi does not mince his words: "Mubarak is responsible for most of the problems of al Qaeda," he said.

Mubarak and al Qaeda

However that claim is judged, what is clear is that many of the Egyptians in Peshawar at the time of al Qaeda's creation in 1988 had been radicalized by harsh treatment in Mubarak's prisons. And Zawahiri's anger against the ally of the regime that imprisoned and tortured him would later help fuel al Qaeda's decision to launch the September 11 attacks [referring to the 2001 terrorist attacks on the United States].

Rushdi says the end of the Mubarak regime will prevent men like Zawahiri from again emerging in Egypt.

Benotman, the former Libyan jihadist, cautions against jumping to such conclusions. He stresses that regime change is far from complete in Tunisia and Egypt. He argues that as long as Western-backed armed forces continue to dominate politics across the region, al Qaeda's message will continue to hit home for some, adding that those who are already ideologically committed to al Qaeda's global jihad are unlikely to be swayed by current events.

The past 10 days demonstrated that events can take unpredictable turns, offering up opportunities for Islamist terrorist groups.

The Case of Libya

In Libya, an ongoing deadly crackdown on protesters could provide an opportunity to al Qaeda and regional affiliates to gain new recruits. Radicalization in recent years has run high in Libya, especially in its eastern provinces. While the Iraqi insurgency was at its peak, more young men traveled from Libya to join al Qaeda in Iraq than from any country apart from Saudi Arabia.

Yemen

As protests sweep the region, nowhere is U.S. national security more at stake than in Yemen, from where al Qaeda in the

Arabian Peninsula has twice launched attempts to attack the U.S. homeland in the last 14 months.

There is a danger that the recent deadly assaults on protesters in Sana'a [the capital of Yemen] by pro-government elements could be exploited by al Qaeda in the Arabian Peninsula in the coming weeks to win recruits for its intensifying campaign against security services in the country, especially if the death toll rises and the protest movement is crushed. President Ali Abdullah Saleh's close counterterrorism cooperation with the United States would allow al Qaeda to weave such a crackdown into its propaganda narrative of American-backed dictatorships oppressing Muslim populations.

There is also a danger that if demonstrations gather force and there is a precipitous and chaotic end to Saleh's 33-year rule, al Qaeda may have, at least in the short term, an opportunity to extend its safe haven in the country.

Bahrain

In the Gulf state of Bahrain, a key U.S. ally hosting the headquarters of the United States Fifth Fleet, any repeat of last week's deadly crackdown on demonstrators could also be exploited by al Qaeda, even if many (but by no means all) of those demonstrating are from the country's majority but disenfranchised-feeling Shiite community. The group has often been targeted by al Qaeda and like-minded groups across the Muslim world because their views are seen as heretical.

Future Opportunities for Jihadists

Benotman says that with the weakening of security services in some Arab countries, the greatest future opportunities may lie for jihadist groups with a narrow regional agenda rather than those like al Qaeda focused on attacking the United States and its Western allies.

According to Benotman, one of the groups that may try to rebuild its activities in Egypt is Zawahiri's very own group: Egyptian Islamic Jihad.

Zawahiri fused his group with al Qaeda shortly before September 11 and aligned it with bin Laden's global jihad, against the desire of some within the group who wanted to carry on focusing on operations in Egypt.

Earlier this month, what appears to be a breakaway faction of Egyptian Islamic Jihad issued a statement on the situation in Egypt, calling for the "elimination of the Pharaoh and his lackeys." The statement was issued from Iran under the name of Tharwat Salah Shehata.

Benotman—who met Shehata, an Egyptian lawyer turned jihadist, in Kandahar, Afghanistan, in 2000—says he was a leading figure in the group in the 1990s.

Shehata, according to Benotman, opposed the group's merger with al Qaeda and vied with Zawahiri for leadership of the group in the years before September 11. Shehata and several other members of Egyptian Islamic Jihad appear to have eventually found safe haven in Iran.

Egyptian Islamic Jihad

The new Egyptian Islamic Jihad statement, says Benotman, represents a relaunching of the group's campaign to create an Islamic state in Egypt. Given the geopolitical standoff between Iran and Egypt, Benotman says it is likely that Iranian authorities gave tacit approval for the group to issue the communiqué.

If Benotman is right, this may be the start of a shift by some Islamist militant groups back toward attempts to topple regimes in the Arab world, weakened by the events of the past weeks.

Some argue that it was the successful repression of jihadist groups by the security forces of Arab regimes that led al Qaeda to target the United States in the first place. Forced into exile in countries like Afghanistan and Pakistan, men like Zawahiri came to view the United States as the main barrier to the creation of new Islamic order at home.

What Is al-Qaeda?

Al-Qaeda, Arabic for "the Base," is an international terrorist network founded by Osama bin Laden in the late 1980s. It seeks to rid Muslim countries of what it sees as the profane influence of the West and replace their governments with fundamentalist Islamic regimes. After al-Qaeda's September 11, 2001, attacks, the United States launched a war in Afghanistan to destroy al-Qaeda's bases there and overthrow the Taliban, the country's Muslim fundamentalist rulers who harbored bin Laden and his followers. Like his predecessor George W. Bush, President Barack Obama has committed U.S. strategy to destroying al-Qaeda's safe haven in the Afghanistan-Pakistan region, and limiting the group's ability to strike U.S. targets.

Jayshree Bajoria and Greg Bruno, "al-Qaeda,"
Council on Foreign Relations, August 29, 2011.

"Mubarak exported Egypt's problems to the whole world," said Rushdi, the former Egyptian jihadist.

Outside Yemen, it may prove difficult for jihadist groups to gain traction. Violent campaigns by Islamist militants in Algeria and Egypt in the 1990s turned the vast majority of the population against them. Furthermore, decades of repression by security services destroyed many jihadist groups' capabilities or restricted them to remote areas like the Sahel region south of Algeria and Egypt's Sinai desert.

Additionally, in some countries, like Libya, reconciliation efforts have reduced the risk of a return to violence because they removed from the scene established jihadist outfits capable of recruiting and organizing radical-leaning youth. Several former members of the Libyan Islamic Fighting Group were released Wednesday as a part of an ongoing peace process initiated by Saif al-Islam Gadhafi, the son of Libya's leader, which saw the group renounce violence in Libya.

What Jihadist Groups Should Fear

But what such jihadist groups should fear most is a real and sustained transition toward democracy, broad-based economic opportunity and freedom of expression in the Arab world. Far fewer young Arabs would probably then be attracted to violent Islamist ideology. Like the protesters of Tahrir Square, they would find meaning, purpose and opportunities in other causes.

Change, of course, will not come overnight. And in some Arab countries, even if pro-democracy demonstrators prevail, political transformation will probably take many years to achieve. Yemen is a case in point because of its weak state institutions, lack of an educated middle class and strong tribal structures. But if there is a pan-Arab political opening, the momentum will be strongly against al Qaeda.

The events in the Arab world may also have an impact on homegrown extremism in the West.

In Europe, radical Islamist preachers have been able to prey on a sense of identity loss, discrimination and alienation experienced by second- and third-generation Muslim immigrants from the Arab world and South Asia. Their message has been that such youngsters should devote themselves to efforts to remove an oppressive Western presence from the Muslim world so that a theocratic Islamic Golden Age can be recreated.

But at a time when images of Tahrir Square rather than American tanks are dominating Al Jazeera and other news outlets popular amongst immigrant communities in Europe, that radical vision may start to lose its luster. Moreover, it will be harder for radical preachers to sell the line that Western-style democracy is inherently anti-Muslim and un-Islamic, if

Arab diaspora communities see it empowering their relatives on the southern shores of the Mediterranean.

The Story of Osama Rushdi

If the winds are indeed changing from an era of Islamist militancy to democracy in the Middle East, nothing is more illustrative of this than the story of Osama Rushdi, the former Egyptian jihadist interviewed for this [viewpoint].

Previously the spokesman of [Al-Gama'a al-Islamiyya], an armed Egyptian jihadist group, Rushdi resigned from the group in the mid-1990s, renounced violence and has in recent years worked closely together with a range of Egyptian opposition figures in the UK, including secular liberal intellectuals under the auspices of the Save Egypt Front to bring constitutional democracy to Egypt. Last year, he even helped organize a conference in London for Mohamed ElBaradei, a Nobel Prize laureate and potential Egyptian presidential candidate, and he now hopes to return to Egypt.

"The Egyptian young people created one of the biggest wonderful peaceful civilian revolutions, so now they are proud about themselves and demand a civilian state and democratic institutions," Rushdi said.

In the long term, a successful democratic transition in the Arab world would arguably make the United States significantly safer from al Qaeda terrorism. The threat of attack would remain because, as September 11 illustrated, even a small group of dedicated individuals can create terrible carnage, and al Qaeda today continues to enjoy safe havens in Pakistan and Yemen from where it can organize new attacks. But if al Qaeda's recruiting efforts are significantly hampered, so will its campaign of global terrorism.

> *"Throughout the Arab world ... homo-sexual conduct remains taboo—it is punishable by floggings, long prison terms and in some cases execution."*

Gays in Egypt, Tunisia Worry About Post-Revolt Era

David Crary

David Crary is a reporter for the Associated Press. In the following viewpoint, he underscores the concern from some human rights activists over the future of gay rights in Arab Spring countries, especially Egypt and Tunisia. Crary reports that activists worry that the increasing popularity and political power of hard-line Islamist groups could mean more intolerance and persecution of gay men and women. Yet there is a lot of long-term optimism and hope that the Arab people will respect the existence of gay people and practice tolerance and acceptance.

As you read, consider the following questions:

1. According to the author, how many Egyptian men were arrested in a police raid on a Nile boat restaurant/disco in 2001 and tried in court for immoral behavior and contempt of religion?

2. What was unusual about Mostafa Fathi's novel, *In the World of Boys*?

3. What kind of magazine does Fathi hope to publish in Egypt, according to the viewpoint?

While many of their compatriots savor a new political era, gays in Egypt and Tunisia aren't sharing the joy, according to activists who wonder if the two revolutions could in fact make things worse for an already marginalized community.

In both countries, gays and their allies worry that conservative Islamists, whose credo includes firm condemnation of homosexuality, could increase their influence in elections later this year.

"Our struggle goes on—it gets more and more difficult," Tunisian gay-rights and HIV-AIDS activist Hassen Hanini wrote to the Associated Press in an e-mail. "The Tunisian gay community is still seeking its place in society in this new political environment."

In much of the world, the push for gay rights has advanced inexorably in recent years. Countries which now allow same-sex marriage range from Portugal to South Africa to Argentina.

Throughout the Arab world, however, homosexual conduct remains taboo—it is punishable by floggings, long prison terms and in some cases execution in religiously conservative Saudi Arabia, and by up to three years imprisonment in relatively secular Tunisia. Iraq and Yemen each experienced a surge of killings of gays two years ago.

In Egypt, consensual same-sex relations are not prohibited as such, but other laws—those prohibiting "debauchery" or "shameless public acts"—have been used to imprison gay men in recent years.

Ten years ago, Egypt attracted worldwide attention—including criticism from international human-rights groups—

when 52 men were arrested in a police raid on a Nile boat restaurant/disco and accused of taking part in a gay sex party. After a highly publicized trial in an emergency state security court, 23 of the men were convicted and sentenced to prison terms of one to five years for immoral behavior and contempt of religion.

The case caused a storm in Egypt as some newspapers published names and photos of the defendants in graphic stories. At the start of the trial, many defendants covered their faces with towels in the presence of photographers.

In 2008, four HIV-positive Egyptians were sentenced to three years in prison after being convicted of the "habitual practice of debauchery." Human-rights groups warned that the case could undermine HIV/AIDS prevention efforts in Egypt.

U.S.-based Human Rights Watch—which monitors discrimination against gays as part of wide-ranging global activities—says there are no organizations in Egypt which specifically identify as gay-rights advocates.

"There's been no movement on this issue in Egypt since the revolution nor is there likely to be any improvement in the short term," said Heba Morayef, the main Egypt researcher for Human Rights Watch.

Some of the void in advocacy is filled by the Egyptian Initiative for Personal Rights, which in a decade of existence has defended people entangled in various anti-gay prosecutions as part of its broader civil-liberties agenda.

The group's executive director, Hossam Bahgat, said the once-common use of entrapment to arrest gays has subsided in recent years. But he said anti-gay debauchery trials still take place occasionally.

Short term, Bahgat was skeptical that any Western-style gay-rights movement could take hold in Egypt—despite the sense of liberation following the February ouster of Hosni Mubarak, the longtime authoritarian president.

Arab Gays Can Work with Islamists

Islamists are social conservatives. But that does not mean that they are necessarily unapproachable or irrational. Furthermore, gay Arabs cannot be cut out of the fabric of their societies; they are Arab, they are Muslim, Christian, conservative and progressive, soldiers and civilians, communists and capitalists, sexist and feminist, classist and revolutionary, and both oppressors and the oppressed. Islamist discourses are not ossified and stuck in the 16th century, as most Western commentators assume. They are plural, responsive, dynamic, and they represent the point of view of a large and diverse public.

Maya Mikdashi and R.M.,
"Gays, Islamists, and the Arab Spring:
What Would a Revolutionary Do?," Jadaliyya,
June 11, 2011. www.jadaliyya.com.

"The challenge is to ensure that what emerges from the transition isn't just a democratic government but also a democratic society," Bahgat said, referring to the quest for equitable treatment of women, religious minorities and gays.

"Any attempt to fixate only on the issue of same-sex relationships is not going to be very fruitful and can cause more harm than good," he said. "We have to learn to coexist, to not only accept our diversity, but even celebrate it."

In the long term, Bahgat said he was cautiously optimistic because Egyptians under 30—a majority of the population—seem more open than their elders to the concept of a diverse Egypt.

"As Egypt moves from dictatorship to being a normal country, we are going to have to live with people we completely disagree with, and there will be elements trying to impose their own understanding of morality," he said. "We're going to win some battles and lose some others."

Notable among the young Egyptians trying to change attitudes toward gays is Mostafa Fathi, 28, the editor in chief at a Cairo-based Internet radio station. Two years ago, he published a book called *In the World of Boys* which he says is the first Egyptian novel depicting a gay central character empathetically.

The book stirred controversy, and Fathi said some government officials made known their displeasure. But it was not banned, and Fathi said copies are still available in some bookstores.

"In my book, I have a character who says, 'I am a gay. You have to respect me,'" Fathi said. "We all should respect everyone. It's not good to judge people as evil."

In contemporary Cairo, the setting for Fathi's book, it's commonly acknowledged that there is a relatively established gay community, perhaps a bit less paranoid than in the past but still operating secretively.

"You have to talk about it under the table," he said. "I like to think the future will be better . . . but most of the Egyptian people still reject gays."

He was surprised that a straightforward article about his book, by a foreign writer, was posted on the English-language web site of the conservative Muslim Brotherhood, Egypt's most powerful political movement. However, Fathi noted that comments on the Brotherhood's Arabic site were virulently critical of his novel, with some saying gays should be killed.

Fathi says he wants to launch an online magazine about gays in Egypt that would include discussion of serious issues such as protection against violence and infectious diseases. A trusted friend who's a human-rights lawyer convinced him to wait for the political situation to stabilize: "He says it's a good idea, but not now. Maybe in a year or two."

Given the nature of his novel, Fathi says he is often asked if he is gay.

"I never say I'm gay or not," he explained. "I say it's none of your business."

Egypt's first post-revolution elections are scheduled for September, and the Muslim Brotherhood is expected to compete for half of the seats in Parliament. In Tunisia, where long-term dictator Zine El Abidine Ben Ali was ousted in January, elections are planned for July, and liberals worry that Islamists may gain power.

Under Ben Ali, Tunisia won some international praise for granting women more rights than most other Arab countries, but otherwise was widely criticized for human-rights abuses. Gays weren't necessarily singled out; much of the repression was aimed at political dissent.

Hanini, the Tunisian activist, said some Tunisian gays became a bit more open about themselves in recent years, but for the most part they were discreet about their socializing. He noted that the country's law against homosexual conduct—Penal Code 230—remains in force.

Hanini says Tunisia's modest corps of gay-rights activists took part in the uprising that led to Ben Ali's ouster but now worry that political developments may work against them.

"The prestige of the state is no longer respected," he wrote. "This doesn't work in favor of Tunisian gays, who are finding it increasingly difficult to be accepted."

"And don't forget the Islamist parties who are trying to play the role of judge right now, and who view homosexuality and the gay community as a product of the former regime," he said. "They call it 'rot' that must be cleaned away."

One of Hanini's fellow activists, Badr Baabou, said in an e-mail that Tunisian gays "face a daily struggle—in the street, at school, in the workplace, in one's family—to be accepted and respected."

The current political atmosphere is tense and uncertain, not only for gays but for the country as a whole, he wrote. Yet he concluded on a hopeful note.

"The image I keep thinking is a mother giving birth to her child, with cries of pain," he said. "Out of this, I think we can grow into a Tunisia that's more modern, open and tolerant."

Periodical and Internet Sources Bibliography

The following articles have been selected to supplement the diverse views presented in this chapter.

Rania Abouzeid	"How the Arab Spring Made Bin Laden an Afterthought," *Time*, May 2, 2011.
Omar Ashour	"The Arab Spring Is Al-Qaeda's Winter," *Daily Star* (Lebanon), September 9, 2011.
Alon Ben-Meir	"The Arab Spring: Political Reforms Must Be Accompanied by Economic Developments," *Huffington Post*, November 1, 2011. www .huffingtonpost.com.
Catriona Davies	"Will Gays Be 'Sacrificial Lambs' in Arab Spring?," CNN.com, May 27, 2011.
Omar Halawa	"Future Uncertain for Al-Qaeda Following Arab Spring," *Egypt Independent*, May 9, 2011.
Jon Jensen	"Osama bin Laden's Demise Began with the Arab Spring," GlobalPost, June 6, 2011. www .globalpost.com.
Tim Lister	"New al Qaeda Message Reinforces Focus on Arab Spring," CNN.com, September 13, 2011.
Robin Morgan	"Women of the Arab Spring," *Ms. Magazine*, Spring 2011.
Manal Omar	"Women in Libya and the Arab Spring," *Huffington Post*, November 4, 2011. www .huffingtonpost.com.
Alexandra Sandels	"An Online 'Arab Spring' for Region's Gays and Lesbians," *Los Angeles Times*, June 19, 2011.

For Further Discussion

Chapter 1

1. This chapter outlines a variety of reasons for the Arab Spring. Read all six viewpoints in the chapter. Which reasons seem the most important, and why?

2. Rami G. Khouri contends that a desire for democracy and social justice sparked the uprisings of the Arab Spring. Leon T. Hadar, however, views those uprisings as a power grab. What do you see as the dangers of the Arab Spring, and how can they be avoided?

3. The role of social media in the Arab Spring has been a hot topic. How would you describe the impact of Twitter, Facebook, and other social media during the protests? Read viewpoints by Johnny West and Evgeny Morozov to inform your answer.

Chapter 2

1. How can the West support a burgeoning democratic awakening in the Middle East? Read all six viewpoints included in the chapter to inform your answer.

2. Ahmed Moor asserts that the international community is right to intervene in Libya. Seumas Milne delineates his opposition to international intervention. Which author makes the more powerful and thorough argument? Which one is the more moral position, and why?

Chapter 3

1. Do you believe the United States should support democratic movements in the Middle East? State your position on the matter and explain your reasoning.

2. Matt Welch contends that the United States should not be intervening in Middle Eastern politics. To what extent do you think the United States has the right to intervene in the region? Justify your position clearly.

Chapter 4

1. In the following chapter on the consequences of the Arab Spring, several viewpoints discuss opportunities while other commentators see dangers. Read all the viewpoints. Which political or social consequence do you feel is the most likely to happen? Which do you perceive as the most dangerous? Explain your reasoning.

2. How has the Arab Spring affected al Qaeda? Paul Cruickshank argues that it makes the group less dangerous. Do you agree with his assessment? Why or why not?

Organizations to Contact

The editors have compiled the following list of organizations concerned with the issues debated in this book. The descriptions are derived from materials provided by the organizations. All have publications or information available for interested readers. The list was compiled on the date of publication of the present volume; the information provided here may change. Be aware that many organizations take several weeks or longer to respond to inquiries, so allow as much time as possible.

Council on Foreign Relations (CFR)
1777 F Street NW, Washington, DC   20006
(202) 509-8400 • fax: (202) 509-8490
website: www.cfr.org

The Council on Foreign Relations (CFR) is an independent, nonprofit membership organization and think tank that focuses on providing accurate, insightful, and provocative analysis and commentary on US foreign policy for government officials, businesspeople, journalists, educators, activists, and civic leaders. CFR features a Studies Program that generates independent research, policy briefs, and analysis and holds roundtable discussions to bring together experts, senior government officials, media pundits and journalists, and policy makers to debate issues and generate concrete policy recommendations and innovative solutions to foreign policy issues. CFR publishes *Foreign Affairs*, a journal on international affairs and foreign policy, as well as a number of policy briefs, analyses, backgrounders, blogs, and expert briefs that can be accessed on the CFR website.

Foundation for Middle East Peace (FMEP)
1761 N Street NW, Washington, DC   20036
(202) 835-3650 • fax: (202) 835-3651

e-mail: info@fmep.org
website: www.fmep.org

The Foundation for Middle East Peace (FMEP) is a nonprofit organization that is dedicated to finding a way to forge a lasting peace between Israel and Palestine. To this end, FMEP offers small grants to support educational, civil rights, recreational, and humanitarian activities that promote peace and a greater understanding of the issues involved in the conflict. Since 1992 FMEP has published the *Report on Israeli Settlements in the Occupied Territories*, a bimonthly periodical that features detailed and insightful analysis on the Israeli-Palestinian issue. Commentary and analysis on a range of topics related to the conflict can be accessed on the FMEP website.

Middle East Institute (MEI)

1761 N Street NW, Washington, DC   20036
(202) 785-1141 • fax: (202) 331-8861
e-mail: information@mei.edu
website: www.mei.edu

The Middle East Institute (MEI) was established in 1946 to provide unbiased and insightful information on the Middle East and facilitate a better understanding of the region for US policy makers, business leaders, and students. MEI hosts lectures and conferences that feature regional experts from around the world and offer a variety of views on topical issues. It also offers accredited classes in Arabic, Hebrew, Persian, and Turkish languages, culture, and history, as well as publishes *The Middle East Journal*, a periodical that includes scholarly research and cogent analysis on Middle East issues.

Middle East Media Research Institute (MEMRI)

PO Box 27837, Washington, DC   20038
(202) 955-9070 • fax: (202) 955-9077
e-mail: memri@memri.org
website: www.memri.org

The Middle East Media Research Institute (MEMRI) is a non-partisan organization dedicated to monitoring the media in the Middle East—television, websites, print, and religious sermons—to better understand the issues important to people and groups in the region and forge an improved understanding of Middle Eastern culture and politics. MEMRI hopes to provide accurate and relevant information to inform the debate on US policy in the Middle East. MEMRI posts clips of television programs, public speeches, sermons, movies, and Internet videos to illuminate attitudes on subjects such as anti-Semitism, Holocaust denial, and global jihad.

Middle East Policy Council (MEPC)

1730 M Street NW, Suite 512, Washington, DC 20036
(202) 296-6767
e-mail: info@mepc.org
website: www.mepc.org

The Middle East Policy Council (MEPC) is a nonprofit educational organization established in 1981 to inform the debate on political, cultural, and economic issues of US interest in the Middle East such as the Arab Spring, the Israel-Palestine conflict, and Islamic fundamentalism and global jihad. MEPC organizes the Capitol Hill conference series, which brings together regional analysts and congressional staffs for a discussion of key political issues. It also publishes *Middle East Policy*, a quarterly journal that reports on and analyzes a wide range of subjects related to the Middle East and US foreign policy in the region. A number of articles and commentary by MEPC scholars can be accessed on the organization's website.

National Council on US-Arab Relations (NCUSAR)

1730 M Street NW, Suite 503, Washington, DC 20036
(202) 293-6466 • fax: (202) 293-7770
website: www.ncusar.org

The National Council on US-Arab Relations (NCUSAR) is a nonprofit educational organization that was established in 1983 to inform American understanding of the Arab world.

NCUSAR offers study-abroad opportunities for eligible students; coordinates the Model Arab League, a program in which students learn about Arab history and geopolitical interests; and oversees the Joseph J. Malone Fellowship in Arab and Islamic Studies. NCUSAR also holds public educational briefings on Capitol Hill to debate and exchange ideas on US foreign policy in the Middle East and ways to improve US-Arab relations. The NCUSAR website features a range of articles, commentaries, policy briefs, videos, and newsletters, including the *Council Chronicle* and *NCUSAR Newsletter*.

National Endowment for Democracy (NED)
1025 F Street NW, Suite 800, Washington, DC   20004
(202) 378-9700 • fax: (202) 378-9407
e-mail: info@ned.org
website: www.ned.org

The National Endowment for Democracy (NED) is a private, nonprofit organization that works to develop and strengthen democratic institutions around the world through financial support and other nonviolent methods. NED provides assistance to trade unions, nongovernmental organizations, political parties, independent media, and business organizations struggling to establish democratic institutions and practices in their area. During the Arab Spring, NED was particularly active reaching out to democratic activists in countries like Tunisia and Egypt. NED publishes the *Journal of Democracy*, a quarterly journal that studies the political struggles for democracy all over the world.

Project on Middle East Democracy (POMED)
1611 Connecticut Avenue NW, Suite 300
Washington, DC   20009
(202) 828-9660
website: www.pomed.org

The Project on Middle East Democracy (POMED) is an independent, nonprofit organization dedicated to fostering democracy in the Middle East and promoting US foreign policies that support a nonviolent democratic awakening in that region. POMED organizes conferences and seminars to encourage dialogue between Americans and Middle Easterners; conducts and disseminates research to legislators, policy makers, and other stakeholders to provide accurate information on countries, politicians, and relevant issues; and offers analyses, policy papers, and in-depth studies that promote democratic reforms in Arab countries. These publications can be accessed on the POMED website, which also offers e-mail updates and newsletters.

US Department of State
2201 C Street NW, Washington, DC   20520
(202) 647-4000
website: www.state.gov

The US Department of State is the federal agency that is responsible for formulating, implementing, and assessing US foreign policy. The State Department also assists US citizens living or traveling abroad; promotes and protects US business interests all over the world; and supports the activities of other US federal agencies in foreign countries. During the Arab Spring, the State Department was very active in enacting diplomatic efforts and informing the US Congress, the president, and the public about the political, economic, and social events in the region. The State Department website features a wealth of information on current policies, upcoming events, daily schedules of top officials, and updates from various countries. It also has video, congressional testimony, speech transcripts, background notes, human rights reports, and strategy reviews.

US Institute of Peace (USIP)
2301 Constitution Avenue NW, Washington, DC   20037
(202) 457-1700 • fax: (202) 429-6063
website: www.usip.org

The US Institute of Peace (USIP) is an independent conflict management center tasked by the US Congress with finding peaceful methods to mitigate international conflicts. USIP strives "to save lives, increase the government's ability to deal with conflicts before they escalate, reduce government costs, and enhance our national security." USIP publishes a number of newsletters for the public, including *PeaceWatch*, which offers information on USIP events and initiatives; the *Conflict Prevention Newsletter*, a bimonthly newsletter that investigates the organization's work mitigating conflict and reports on its special projects; and *Publications and Tools Weekly*, which recaps the latest international developments. The website also provides access to webcasts, videos, and audio.

Bibliography of Books

Sohrab Ahmari and Nasser Weddady, eds.
Arab Spring Dreams: The Next Generation Speaks Out for Freedom and Justice from North Africa to Iran. New York: Palgrave Macmillan, 2012.

John R. Bradley
After the Arab Spring: How the Islamists Hijacked the Middle East Revolts. New York: Palgrave Macmillan, 2012.

Erik A. Claessen
Stalemate: An Anatomy of Conflicts Between Democracies, Islamists, and Muslim Autocrats. Santa Barbara, CA: Praeger, 2010.

Judith Cochran
Democracy in the Middle East: The Impact of Religion and Education. Lanham, MD: Lexington Books, 2011.

Fred Dallmayr
The Promise of Democracy: Political Agency and Transformation. Albany: State University of New York Press, 2010.

Nonie Darwish
The Devil We Don't Know: The Dark Side of Revolutions in the Middle East. Hoboken, NJ: Wiley, 2012.

Bruce Feiler
Generation Freedom: The Middle East Uprisings and the Remaking of the Modern World. New York: William Morrow, 2011.

Lloyd C. Gardner   *The Road to Tahrir Square: Egypt and the United States from the Rise of Nasser to the Fall of Mubarak.* New York: New Press, 2011.

Reuel Marc Gerecht   *The Wave: Man, God, and the Ballot Box in the Middle East.* Stanford, CA: Hoover Institution Press, 2011.

Roger Hardy   *The Muslim Revolt: A Journey Through Political Islam.* New York: Columbia University Press, 2010.

Mark Hitchcock   *Middle East Burning.* Eugene, OR: Harvest House Publishers, 2012.

Irfan Husain   *Fatal Faultlines: Pakistan, Islam and the West.* Rockville, MD: Arc Manor, 2012.

Matthew F. Jacobs   *Imagining the Middle East: The Building of an American Foreign Policy, 1918–1967.* Chapel Hill: University of North Carolina Press, 2011.

Bernard Lewis   *The End of Modern History in the Middle East.* Stanford, CA: Hoover Institution Press, 2011.

Mahmood Monshipouri, ed.   *Human Rights in the Middle East: Frameworks, Goals, and Strategies.* New York: Palgrave Macmillan, 2011.

Walid Phares   *The Coming Revolution: Struggle for Freedom in the Middle East.* New York: Threshold Editions, 2010.

Nir Rosen

Aftermath: Following the Bloodshed of America's Wars in the Muslim World. New York: Nation Books, 2010.

Barry Rubin, ed.

The Muslim Brotherhood: The Organization and Policies of a Global Islamist Movement. New York: Palgrave Macmillan, 2010.

Barry Rubin, ed.

Security and Stability in the Middle East: Critical Concepts in Military, Strategic and Security Studies. New York: Routledge, 2012.

Hans Schattle

Globalization and Citizenship. Lanham, MD: Rowman & Littlefield Publishers, 2012.

Dina Shehata

Islamists and Secularists in Egypt: Opposition, Conflict, and Cooperation. New York: Routledge, 2010.

Samer S. Shehata, ed.

Islamic Politics in the Middle East: Movements and Change. New York: Routledge, 2011.

Michael J. Totten

The Road to Fatima Gate: The Beirut Spring, the Rise of Hezbollah, and the Iranian War Against Israel. New York: Encounter Books, 2011.

Robin Wright

Rock the Casbah: Rage and Rebellion Across the Islamic World. New York: Simon & Schuster, 2011.

Rami Zurayk

Food, Farming, and Freedom: Sowing the Arab Spring. Charlottesville, VA: Just World Books, 2011.

Index

Temp CB 5/14

ML   I-13